IT HAPPENED TO ME

Series Editor: Arlene Hirschfelder

Books in the It Happened to Me series are designed for inquisitive teens digging for answers about certain illnesses, social issues, or lifestyle interests. Whether you are deep into your teen years or just entering them, these books are gold mines of up-to-date information, riveting teen views, and great visuals to help you figure out stuff. Besides special boxes highlighting singular facts, each book is enhanced with the latest reading lists, websites, and an index. Perfect for browsing, there are loads of expert information by acclaimed writers to help parents, guardians, and librarians understand teen illness, tough situations, and lifestyle choices.

1. *Epilepsy: The Ultimate Teen Guide,* by Kathlyn Gay and Sean McGarrahan, 2002.
2. *Stress Relief: The Ultimate Teen Guide,* by Mark Powell, 2002.
3. *Learning Disabilities: The Ultimate Teen Guide,* by Penny Hutchins Paquette and Cheryl Gerson Tuttle, 2003.
4. *Making Sexual Decisions: The Ultimate Teen Guide,* by L. Kris Gowen, 2003.
5. *Asthma: The Ultimate Teen Guide,* by Penny Hutchins Paquette, 2003.
6. *Cultural Diversity—Conflicts and Challenges: The Ultimate Teen Guide,* by Kathlyn Gay, 2003.
7. *Diabetes: The Ultimate Teen Guide,* by Katherine J. Moran, 2004.
8. *When Will I Stop Hurting? Teens, Loss, and Grief: The Ultimate Teen Guide to Dealing with Grief,* by Ed Myers, 2004.
9. *Volunteering: The Ultimate Teen Guide,* by Kathlyn Gay, 2004.
10. *Organ Transplants—A Survival Guide for the Entire Family: The Ultimate Teen Guide,* by Tina P. Schwartz, 2005.
11. *Medications: The Ultimate Teen Guide,* by Cheryl Gerson Tuttle, 2005.
12. *Image and Identity—Becoming the Person You Are: The Ultimate Teen Guide,* by L. Kris Gowen and Molly C. McKenna, 2005.
13. *Apprenticeship: The Ultimate Teen Guide,* by Penny Hutchins Paquette, 2005.
14. *Cystic Fibrosis: The Ultimate Teen Guide,* by Melanie Ann Apel, 2006.
15. *Religion and Spirituality in America: The Ultimate Teen Guide,* by Kathlyn Gay, 2006.
16. *Gender Identity: The Ultimate Teen Guide,* by Cynthia L. Winfield, 2007.

PREGNANCY AND PARENTING

THE ULTIMATE TEEN GUIDE

JESSICA AKIN

IT HAPPENED TO ME, NO. 48

ROWMAN & LITTLEFIELD
Lanham • Boulder • New York • London

Published by Rowman & Littlefield
A wholly owned subsidiary of The Rowman & Littlefield Publishing Group, Inc.
4501 Forbes Boulevard, Suite 200, Lanham, Maryland 20706
www.rowman.com

Unit A, Whitacre Mews, 26-34 Stannary Street, London SE11 4AB

British Library Cataloguing in Publication Information Available

Library of Congress Cataloging-in-Publication Data

Names: Akin, Jessica, 1983– author.
Title: Pregnancy and parenting : the ultimate teen guide / Jessica Akin.
Description: Lanham : Rowman & Littlefield, [2016] | Series: It happened to me ; 48 | Includes
    bibliographical references and index.
Identifiers: LCCN 2015042078 (print) | LCCN 2015045271 (ebook) | ISBN 9781442243026
    (hardback : alk. paper) | ISBN 9781442243033 (electronic)
Subjects: LCSH: Teenage parents—Juvenile literature. | Teenage pregnancy—Juvenile
    literature.
Classification: LCC HQ759.64 .A395 2016 (print) | LCC HQ759.64 (ebook) | DDC
    362.7/8743—dc23
LC record available at http://lccn.loc.gov/2015042078

♾™ The paper used in this publication meets the minimum requirements of American
National Standard for Information Sciences—Permanence of Paper for Printed Library
Materials, ANSI/NISO Z39.48-1992.

Printed in the United States of America

To teen parents.
May you find the strength, love, and inspiration to see you through
one of life's toughest, most exhausting, and yet often most
rewarding journeys—raising a child.

Contents

Acknowledgments

I want to thank all the teen parents who, with such courage, honesty, and bravery, shared their stories so others could learn and be inspired: Sammi, Billy, Thuy, Mark, Holly, and Monica.

To Ann Angel for always pushing me to honor and trust my own journey. Thank you for being one of my biggest champions and someone I look up to and admire.

To Amanda Angel for helping a fellow writer and author even while it was probably the last thing on your mind. Your generosity and kindness in sharing your story touched my heart.

To all the medical professionals and individuals dedicating their practices to helping teen parents, especially Dr. Gaebler-Uhing, Melissa Vukovich, Barbara Bell, and Tara LaBerge. I hope the time each of you took to sit down and talk with me about how to encourage, uplift, and support teen parents is honored and manifested in this book, as I could not have written it without your words and expertise.

To the best friends anyone could possibly have, who supported me at every step of my journey, listened to my writing woes, and are always available to discuss the dysfunction, disorder, and many delights of parenting and life: Erin, Andy S., Senator, Sara, Kami, Tracy, Jessica K., and Heather.

Finally, to my lovies. Mom and Dad, thank you for all the sacrifices you made and all the support you gave. Jason, thank you for thinking writers and stay-at-home moms, not marketing executives, are hot and for pushing me to try a new career. We really are having a blast, paddling our canoe together. Sophia, Elwood, and Shepherd: Thank you for making my life a richer, funnier, and more exciting place to exist.

Introduction

You didn't wait. You didn't use contraception . . . or even know what constitutes "contraception." You used a condom and it failed. He withdrew, but not quickly enough. You hadn't even gotten your period yet. You were abused. Maybe you are in love and thought having a baby would make your relationship even stronger. Many of you may have no idea how your life ended up here.

Pregnant and a Teen

You're not alone. According to the Alan Guttmacher Institute in 2013, approximately 900,000 teenage girls become pregnant in the United States every year.[1] Almost all of these pregnancies are unplanned, leaving teen moms and dads just like you unprepared for the emotional, physical, and psychological journey ahead of them. Pregnancy and having a baby, whether planned or not, can be one of the most memorable and potentially life-altering moments. Although a supportive family can help teens cope with new responsibilities and social service agencies can offer ideas and ways to finish school and seek employment, this book acts as a guide to help teens—just like you—navigate the unique issues and struggles they alone face throughout a pregnancy.

Any choice a pregnant teen makes comes with a price—a social, emotional, and physical price. Even a quick scan of the various sites that offer resources and awareness related to teen pregnancy—the very sites that announce they are "sources of information" and "guides"—come with a stigma. If you look close enough at several websites designed to support and educate teen parents, you'll catch a faint hint of judgment and criticism woven throughout their content. Take for example the "Letter to Teen Parents" posted on the National Campaign to Prevent Teen and Unplanned Pregnancy's teen-focused website that publically admits the content on its site may insult teen parents: "We know that you work very hard to support yourself and your children, and we think it's great that you've come here to get more information. We also know that our message might unintentionally offend teen parents—that is absolutely not our intent. While we know many of your experiences as a teen parent have been positive, we also know that you understand the difficulties and challenges that come along with parenthood."[2] While this disclaimer might seem derogatory in and of itself, it was actually edited from a previous version that was even more anti–teen parent. However, while the National Campaign to Prevent Teen and Unplanned Pregnancy has since taken the more pointed message down in favor of its current one, the older message is still featured on several other teen pregnancy-focused websites: "If you're already a teen parent, all the stuff on this page might sound like it's meant to hurt your feelings. We know that our message might unintentionally offend teen parents and we hope that you don't take what we're saying here the wrong way. While your experiences as a teen parent may be very positive, we know that the majority of teen moms and dads have an incredibly difficult road ahead for themselves and for their children. We are by no means trying to insult you as a teen parent or make you feel like you've made a bad choice, but are instead hoping to help all teens realize the consequences of having children too early."[3] Although the people behind the sites offer stats, stories, and facts to hopefully persuade teens from ending up in the often undesirable situation of facing an unplanned pregnancy *and* apologize to teen parents for the often perceived negativity of their content, it stands to reason that teen parents coming to the site for help are often not only not helped, but also leave feeling badly about themselves.

That's a rather bold statement. Others are subtler. Head on over to the In the Know Zone website which markets itself as a "one-stop resource for information

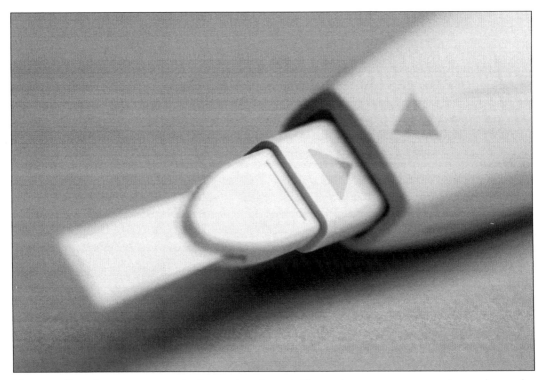

The results of a pregnancy test can be devastating when a pregnancy is unplanned—especially for teens. However, it doesn't have to be. Teen moms and dads can overcome the odds and challenges of parenting.

on substance abuse, sexual, and mental health issues." Even their take on teen pregnancy is wrought with negatively biased stats like, "Poverty is almost inevitable for an unmarried teenage mother," "The economic impact of teen pregnancy is enormous," and "The human cost is incalculable."[4]

There are times where pregnant teen mothers, or soon-to-be fathers, feel as if they are not entitled to a happy pregnancy or parenting experience. It's almost as if "we," as a concerned body of adults and individuals, are trying so hard to prevent teen pregnancies that we forget to address the unique challenges teens face that adults might not. Understandably, this book is not advocating for teen pregnancy. It's a difficult and oftentimes devastating experience for teen moms and dads. This book provides teens dealing with an unexpected pregnancy with resources and insight into issues and concerns very much unique to them, like parenting while finishing high school, understanding the importance of prenatal care, and balancing adult responsibilities of caring for a child while still living at home as a minor.

This isn't a how-to, textbook, or instructional manual. There are many books and resources available online and at local bookstores that cover topics such as pregnancy symptoms, due date calculations, fetal growth and development, morning sickness, diet, weight gain, labor and delivery, fitness, preparing for baby, and more in incredible detail.

This book is for teen mothers and fathers who want to break the perception that having a baby as a teen pretty much translates to being uneducated, on welfare, or as a teen father, not involved in the lives of moms and babies. In this book, you'll follow stories of teens starting from when they realize they are pregnant and continuing through their experiences being a pregnant high schooler, handling lost friends, going to college, and trying to be great moms and dads. The intent of this book is to provide a new road map through true-life stories that educate, impact, and inspire teen parents. The hope for this book is that it actually meets teens where they are emotionally by informing and engaging them through real-life events, facts and statistics, poems, book reviews, and

Try This!

• Having a baby gives you the opportunity to branch outside yourself and your comfort zone to try out new ways of thinking, communicating with others, and learning new skills. Throughout this book are several Try This! tips. Each Try This! tip provides an idea or activity from well-respected experts and resources to encourage a more positive pregnancy experience.

commentary on pop culture to provide support without criticism and help teens learn from their peers.

Because, once teens make a choice—parenting, adoption, or abortion—they often find themselves alone and without any clear way to navigate the many changes they are about to face.

SEX MYTHS

Teens often maintain skewed views and perceptions on the definition of *sex*. This chapter will explore common teen-specific misconceptions and assumptions surrounding sex, including various myths surrounding female and male birth control methods, what it actually takes to get pregnant, what stops pregnancy (no, drinking Mountain Dew will not prevent pregnancy), and who pressures who (it's not always males that pressure and they aren't always the ones "ready" to have sex).

What Do You Think?

"Sex is sex. I don't consider oral sex 'sex' because it's not. I think everyone else feels the same way," says Sammi, an eighteen-year-old teen mom of one child.[1] Sammi was a sixteen-year-old sophomore when she started having sex with Billy, her boyfriend and now father of their daughter. She was seventeen and he was

Just What Is *Sex*?

Is vaginal penetration sex? What about anal penetration, oral sex, petting, and rubbing? What about homosexuals? Are they considered virgins? Confused? You're not alone. Ninety-five percent of people feel that sex is only vaginal penetration by a penis.[a] But, 11 percent believe that if the guy didn't ejaculate, then it wasn't really sex.[b] Another 30 percent believe oral sex and 20 percent believe anal sex are not truly sex.[c] The *Merriam-Webster Dictionary* defines sex as heterosexual intercourse involving penetration of the vagina by the penis and anal or oral intercourse that does not involve penetration of the vagina by the penis.[d]

Complete abstinence is the only 100 percent sure way to not get pregnant. To be blunt: anytime a penis penetrates a vagina, there is a risk of pregnancy. Teens can minimize the risk of not only pregnancy, but also contracting any sexually transmitted diseases, by using at least one form of birth control—like a condom—each and every time they engage in sexual activity.

nineteen when they had their daughter. Sammi, like many teens and even some young adults, knew the risks of unprotected sex but didn't actually believe it would happen to her. Many teens don't even realize that there *is* potential for pregnancy and sexually transmitted infections every time they have unprotected sex.

In Sammi's case, however, her unplanned pregnancy wasn't from a lack of knowing about the risks or even a lack of knowing about the options out there to prevent pregnancy; it was a lack of access to birth control: "I just flat out told my mom that I was planning on having sex and asked to be put on birth control. There's really no point in sneaking around it because it is a positive measure, not a negative."[2] Sammi's mom did not agree with Sammi going on birth control and said no to Sammi's request. While Sammi did have access to condoms, they were not a viable option due to her sensitivity to the latex and other materials used to manufacture them.

Test your beliefs and assumptions about sex by checking out some popular misconceptions and myths about sex.

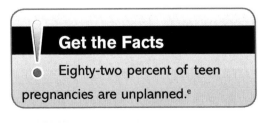

Get the Facts

Eighty-two percent of teen pregnancies are unplanned.[e]

Surprisingly, many teens disagree about what the literal meaning of *having sex* is, and their definitions of what constitutes having sex can range from heavy petting to vaginal penetration.

Myth 1: Everyone is doing it! Sammi absolutely disagrees. "The myth that everyone is doing it just isn't true, and if you're going to choose to have sex just because you think everyone else is, there are a few issues within yourself that you need to sort out first—the LAST of them being your sex life."[3] The stats are on Sammi's side. According to the National Campaign to Prevent Teen and Unplanned Pregnancy, less than half of all high school students have ever had sex.[4]

Myth 2: Guys are always ready and always instigate sex. Wrong—two out of three guys say they'd rather have a relationship without sex, and one in five guys say they've been pressured by a girl to go further sexually than they wanted to. "The myth about girls pressuring guys and vice versa isn't true either. It takes two to tango and it seems that males are always responsible, but the reality is that girls can be just as persistent," says Sammi.[5]

Myth 3: Drinking and drugs make sex much more fun. Actually, what drinking and drugs do is lower an individual's inhibitions, which means teens are more likely to have sex against their better judgment. Twenty percent of teens fifteen to seventeen years old say they have done something sexual while using alcohol or drugs that they might not have done if they were sober.[6]

Myth 4: You can't get pregnant . . . the first time you have sex, when you have your period, if you've never had your period, if you douche, if you drink Mountain

Dew, if you have sex standing up/sitting down/on your side, if you have sex in a hot tub/shower, if you're super skinny, if the guy withdraw . . . the list goes on.

"Thinking you can't get pregnant the first time you have sex is just naive and uneducated. If you think that, it just proves that you aren't at the mental capacity to even have sex at all," says Sammi, who admits this may seem harsh, but she feels that teens must take precautions and make informed decisions since it's not just their life that will be affected but also the lives of everyone involved.[7]

Myth 5: You can skip birth control pills, you can take someone else's, and/or you can double up on birth control pills the morning after to prevent pregnancy. "Taking a birth control pill only right before you have sex is NOT EFFECTIVE. The pill needs to be taken every single day, on time," says Sammi.[8] Sammi is correct to disagree with this myth. Birth control pills are individualized and what works for a friend may not work well for you. Birth control pills are also only effective when used correctly. In fact, they are more than 99 percent effective when taken correctly![9] But taking your friend's, doubling up, or skipping pills decreases their effectiveness in preventing pregnancy and increases the likelihood of an unexpected pregnancy.

Myth 6: You can reuse condoms or use plastic baggies instead of a condom. Sammi was not impressed with this myth: "Besides the fact that reusing a condom is literally disgusting, it is also extremely stupid. Condoms are for one time use only."[10] This myth is referring to male condoms, which are placed over the penis. There are also female condoms, which are inserted into the vagina. We'll stick to male condoms while busting this myth. While male condoms are 98 percent effective at preventing pregnancy, they have to be used correctly.[11] This means condoms must be put on before you start having sex, kept on until you're done, and should never be reused.[12] Unlike plastic baggies, plastic wrap, or other non-condom materials, condoms are made from a variety of materials like latex, polyisoprene, polyurethane, and even lambskin.[13] These materials are specifically designed to protect against unwanted pregnancies by preventing semen from coming into contact with the vagina or vulva. Worried about the condom breaking or falling off during sex? Use both a condom and another birth control method to be safe.

Myth 7: Contraceptives can prevent pregnancy 100 percent. Wrong. No birth control touts a 100 percent success rate. Abstinence (not having sex) is the only 100 percent way to prevent pregnancy. That's because anytime—regardless of the time of month, when teens took their last birth control pill, or if teens use two forms of birth control like spermicide and condoms—semen gets inside the vagina or vulva, women can get pregnant.[14] Sammi agrees. "You can get pregnant ANY TIME you have sex. The only way to properly protect yourself from pregnancy is to use contraception or just not have sex," says Sammi.[15]

She continues, "It's not that there were any myths that I believed and that I was being stupid/uninformed about having sex, it's just that what happened [getting pregnant] was a true accident. People who believe any of those foolish myths are CRAZY and are totally asking for it."[16]

There are a lot of myths out there, and this list doesn't begin to cover the many misconceptions and misinformation teens have about sex, birth control, and preventing unwanted pregnancies. The best thing teens can do is help themselves by getting informed and educating themselves about safe sex practices.

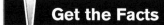

Get the Facts

● Of those teen mothers who were not married when their child was born, only about 34 percent went on to marry by the time their child reached age five.[f]

Am I Ready?

There are many important things to consider when deciding whether sex is the right next step, including your personal values and goals, defining the kinds of emotional and physical risks you're willing to take, if this is really something you want, and the type of relationship you want from the person you're having sex with.

When Sammi reflects about when she decided to have sex, she knows now that she would make a different choice. "Honestly I wasn't ready. If I could choose to be a virgin again, I would. I don't think any young person who decides to have sex is ready because almost all of us regret it at one point or another."[17]

Take some time to do a little inner reflection and push yourself to answer the following questions honestly—whether you're currently having sex or thinking about it for the first time:

- How does your family feel about sex? Have you talked with your parents about wanting to have sex? If no, why not?
- How does your religion or spiritual code respond to sex before marriage and sex as a teenager?
- Are you in a long-term, monogamous relationship? If not, do you want to be in one before you have sex?
- Have you and your partner discussed the risks of sexually transmitted infections and pregnancy openly together? If no, why not?
- Have you and your partner agreed on the method of contraceptives or birth control you both are going to use? If no, why not?

- Have you discussed with your primary health care professional that you are intending to start having sex? If no, why not?
- How would you handle a sexually transmitted infection or pregnancy?
- Do you feel like you need to have sex because "everyone" is having sex?
- Do you feel like your partner will leave you if you don't have sex?
- Have you discussed with your partner what intimacy means to both of you and how having sex will impact your relationship? If no, why not?

These are just a few questions to consider. If having sex reflects your values and what's most important to you, you may be ready. If you are prepared to protect yourself against the risks of sex, you may be ready. However, if at any point in this reflection you have a hard time being honest about your responses to these questions or feel like you can't talk openly with your family, friends, partner, or health care professional, you may not be ready.

Sammi's three-year-old daughter is a 24/7 reminder of how difficult, and rewarding, parenting can be. Because of this, Sammi needs zero reminders when it comes to growing her family at this time. "I'm on the pill and it works very well for me. After I had [my daughter] I got terrible acne and the pill cleared that right up! It's nice knowing exactly when my period will come and end, and it's not hard to keep up with it when you realize the importance of doing so."[18]

Being able to be clear about what you want, protect yourself from pregnancy or sexually transmitted infections, and talk about your desires with someone you trust is difficult and can feel overwhelming, but all are important elements of ensuring you are making good decisions regarding your sexual health and freedom.

AM I PREGNANT?

Pregnancy is a complicated process and while many teens experience pregnancy symptoms shortly after ovulation, others notice symptoms once they miss their period. Symptoms such as changes in appetite, weight gain, nausea, and cramping could easily be overlooked or cast off as something other than a pregnancy. Understanding the physical and psychological implications of *actually* being pregnant may help diminish worries teen moms and dads have about *potentially* being pregnant. Although there are many helpful insights in this chapter, if you think you could be pregnant, the best route is to immediately seek counsel and medical attention.

Before we go any further and discuss early and advanced signs of pregnancy, it may be helpful to understand some of the terminology you're about to encounter either in this book or at your prenatal appointments:

- *Egg:* A lot of women refer to what's in their ovaries as eggs, but in fact, those cells we often think of as eggs are called ova. An ovum isn't considered an egg until it's been fertilized by sperm.
- *Embryo:* From the moment the ovum is fertilized by sperm until about the third month of pregnancy what's in a woman's womb is considered an *embryo*. After the beginning of the third month, the embryo is considered a fetus. [1]
- *Estrogen:* This female steroid hormone is produced primarily by the ovaries. Estrogen influences the course of ovulation in monthly menstrual cycles, lactation after pregnancy (a.k.a. breastfeeding), aspects of mood, and aging.
- *Fertilized:* On average, males ejaculate 250 million sperm during intercourse. [2] These little swimmers work their way from the vagina through the cervix, up into the uterus and into the fallopian tube where their sole goal is to penetrate the ovum. Only about 400 sperm will survive the arduous ten-hour journey to the ovum and only one can fertilize it. The process of the sperm penetrating the ovum is fertilization, and it takes roughly twenty minutes for that one sperm to wiggle its way in.
- *Fetus:* From the embryo stage until birth, an unborn baby is called a fetus. [3]

- *Hormones:* These are the chemical substances produced in the body that control and regulate the activity of certain cells or organs.[4] Human chorionic gonadotropin, progesterone, and estrogen are three key hormones in fetal development.[5]
- *Human Chorionic Gonadotropin (HCG):* HCG is the key hormone present during pregnancy produced by what ultimately becomes the placenta. Its basic job is to tell a woman's body that there is a life form growing in her womb and that her body needs to build a nest for it.[6]
- *Menstrual cycle:* This cycle involves the monthly changes in the ovaries and uterus as the body prepares for fertilization. Unless pregnancy occurs and the ovum is fertilized, the cycle ends with the shedding of part of the inner mucus membrane lining the uterus. The shedding is considered menstruation, or getting your period.
- *Ovaries:* The ovaries produce the ova.

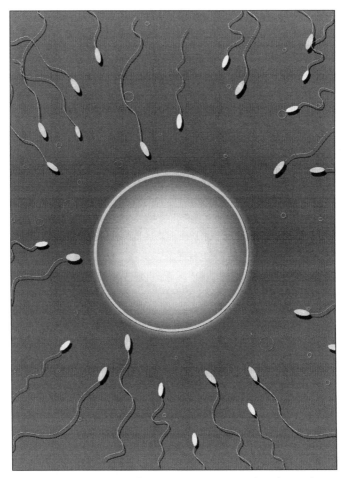

The race is on! From the moment a man ejaculates, hundreds of millions of sperm vie to cross the finish line of penetrating the female's ovum. Conception occurs when the ovum is fertilized by one sperm.

- *Ovulation:* This is the process in which the ovum is released from the ovaries and travels into a woman's fallopian tube.[7] Ovulation usually occurs in the midpoint of a woman's menstrual cycle.
- *Ovum:* The female reproductive cell capable of developing into a new individual is called the ovum.
- *Prenatal:* This term refers to pregnancy, pregnant woman, and birth.[8] Appointments for mom and baby are typically called prenatal appointments.
- *Progesterone:* This hormone keeps the uterus muscle relaxed and plays a role in the immune system helping the body tolerate foreign DNA (a.k.a. the embryo/fetus/baby).
- *Uterus:* The uterus, also commonly known as the womb, is a hollow muscular organ of the female reproductive system that is responsible for the development of the embryo and fetus during pregnancy.[9]

Of course, there are many other terms, phrases, and definitions helpful to understanding what's going on inside while a woman is pregnant, including understanding how the female reproductive system actually works. Many books—such as *What to Expect When You're Expecting* (2008) by Arlene Eisenberg, Heidi Murkoff, and Sharon Mazel; *Your Pregnancy Week by Week* (2011) by Glade Curtis and Judith Schuler; and the *Mayo Clinic Guide to a Healthy Pregnancy: From Doctors Who Are Parents, Too!* (2011)—are dedicated to the biology and physiology of pregnancy. They can be indispensable resources providing a month-by-month breakdown of what to expect as the body changes and baby grows, how the female brain operates, and the macro and micro impact of female hormones during menstrual cycles and pregnancy.

Signs of Pregnancy

Every individual is unique; for some women, pregnancy symptoms can begin almost immediately after conception due to the influx of the hormones estrogen, progesterone, and HCG needed to create and sustain a pregnancy. Although there are many signs and indications you could be pregnant, the best way to ultimately know for sure is a test from your health care provider.

Missed Period

Possibly the earliest external sign of a pregnancy is a missed period, but not always. Many teens don't experience regular cycles the first few years of their menstrual cycles, until their hormone levels stabilize.[10] Many other factors like excessive weight loss or gain, stress, illness, drug or alcohol use, and certain medications can cause a missed period or a period so light it goes by unnoticed.[11]

Nausea and Food Aversions or Cravings

Commonly known as morning sickness, nausea is often attributed to pregnancy. However, that sensation of feeling like you're about to throw up can also be caused by food poisoning or the flu. Pregnant women can also experience food aversions, specifically to the smells of food, and cravings very early on in their pregnancy.

Battling Morning Sickness

Although not the technical medical term for nausea during pregnancy, morning sickness is commonly accepted as the explanation for feeling like you're going to throw up and are just physically spent. Morning sickness's wrath is really based on the individual. Some women never experience that sickly, about-to-toss-your-cookies feeling, while other women feel sick throughout their entire pregnancy. According to BabyCenter.com, this condition affects about three quarters of pregnant women during the first trimester. About half of pregnant women suffer from both nausea and vomiting, one quarter have nausea alone, and one quarter hit the jackpot and aren't affected.[a]

Morning sickness usually starts around six weeks into pregnancy, but it can begin as early as four weeks and tends to ramp up and make preggies feel even more terrible over the next month of their pregnancy. There is some good news, though, for those suffering: about half of the women who get nausea during pregnancy feel complete relief by about fourteen weeks.[b]

But what's a girl (or guy caring for his pregnant companion) to do? Fortunately, there are quite a few medical and holistic options you can consider:

- Forgo having three square meals a day and focus on eating small, frequent snack-like meals of around two hundred calories throughout the day. Consider having toast and a piece of fruit for breakfast, celery with peanut butter for a midmorning snack, a hard-boiled egg and chicken breast for lunch, some nuts and another piece of fruit for a midafternoon snack, maybe pasta with veggies and lean protein for dinner, and end your night with a bowl of gelatin, fruit, or yogurt. Crackers and saltines are also really great staples to have on hand if you're feeling you can't stomach anything else.

- Drink lots of water and limit your caffeine intake.
- Avoid smells that might trigger your nausea. Bacon, coffee, strong perfumes, and other scents could really throw you off and bring on a bout of vomiting. BabyCenter.com suggests taking this a step further and experimenting with aromatherapy.[c] Try identifying smells that you enjoy and incorporating either essential oils or candles into your living space to diffuse more palatable scents.
- Rest. Nausea can be exacerbated when you're tired or not getting enough sleep. If possible, sleep in a little later, go to bed an hour earlier, or even try to get a twenty-minute nap into your day.
- Exercise. Perhaps a ten-mile run isn't in order, but getting outside in the fresh air and taking a walk has helped many pregnant women when they are being plagued by morning sickness.
- Take your prenatal vitamins. What are these, you might be wondering? These are vitamins specifically designed for the pregnant woman and the baby growing within her.
- Try ginger. Ginger is a homeopathic remedy popular for its ability to settle stomach queasiness. Try grating fresh ginger into hot water, ginger candies, or even ginger ale.

If you're not finding anything that helps, talk to your medical professional right away. He or she may have alternative options and medicines and also will have a better and more specific understanding of your situation in order to best diagnose and understand where your nausea is coming from.

Tender, Swollen Breasts

Pregnant women can notice achy, tingly, and slightly swollen feelings in their breasts as early as two to three weeks after ovulation, which is typically right before you'd expect to get your next period.

Morning sickness symptoms like a pounding headache, nausea and vomiting, and exhaustion might feel like a hangover when in fact the teen is expecting.

Exhaustion and Headaches

Due to the number of physical changes taking place in the body to support the growth of the baby, including the influx of hormones, pregnant women can feel intense levels of tiredness, fatigue, and headaches.

Slight Bleeding or Cramping

Experiencing what seems like a lighter period could also be implementation bleeding. This happens very early after ovulation when the fertilized egg attaches itself to the uterine wall.

Moodiness

The rollercoaster of emotions pregnant women experience may in fact be due to the rising levels of hormones needed to support the growth of the baby.

Dizziness

Either low blood sugar or blood vessels dilating and blood pressure dropping can create a sense of room-spinning vertigo.

Frequent Urination

Getting up several times a night to pee? Having to use the bathroom often could be caused by the growing uterus pressing against the bladder. Although this typically heightens in the latter stages of pregnancy, many women experience the increased need to go within the first few weeks of their pregnancy.

His Point of View

Billy found out his girlfriend was pregnant via a text message. "I didn't know she was pregnant until she texted me while I was at work one night. She never got sick. She was the perfect pregnant woman. No fatigue, diabetes, and no depression."[d]

Billy came from a well-adjusted, two-parent, middle-class family, but he wasn't a happy kid, struggled in school, and acted out. "I always had a dream of jumping on the train and going off the grid. I wanted to pack my bags and leave. I was raised better than I acted and I didn't care. Life was just a thirty case a night."

Billy was seventeen when he first started having sex. His girlfriend, Sammi from chapter 1, was not his first. Before his daughter, Billy was literally on the verge of going to prison. He had been convicted of a felony for physical endangerment with a vehicle after jumping hills and having a girl in the back seat break her back due to not wearing a seatbelt. "I drank heavily and did drugs. I hid everything and the partying from my girlfriend. I was frightened that if I hit something or crashed, I'd be walking or dead since I never brought my phone." Given his erratic behavior and his overall focus primarily on himself, it didn't surprise him to find out via a text message that his girlfriend was pregnant. Finding out he was going to be a father also wasn't a catalyst for him to change his bad-boy ways.

After serving his sentence for his felony, Billy was in and out of jail for not paying tickets, driving on a revoked license, and a smattering of other infractions. These bad decisions he largely credits to his drug and alcohol usage. "When my daughter was first born, I still used, but didn't drink. I cracked down on being a family man. It's just when I was home, since my daughter didn't live with me, I'd go out at night and smoke. But, I always got caught."

Billy wanted to change, wanted to be a good father. He understood the responsibility and deeply loved his daughter. "I was a rough and tough person. Always in fights to solve problems. When I took my daughter for the first time to a car show, the Vera Bradley bag filled with snacks, someone came up to me and said, 'I never would have seen you as a loving dad.' People didn't believe I could change and that I wasn't an idiot anymore." It meant a lot to Billy to be seen and respected for getting straight, but it was harder than he ever thought possible after so many years and deeply ingrained bad habits.

When his daughter turned two, Billy was again finding it difficult to stay sober. "I always wanted to be clean and be there for her and not worry about being high picking her up—or getting that phone call that she needs help and being so messed up that I couldn't."

He started going to school at a local technical college for welding. "Having a baby made me go to school. You need an education to support another being. You gotta make money somehow." However, because he was in and out of jail, he couldn't make classes and stay gainfully employed for any length of time, which made it hard to continue his schooling.

Billy is currently living out of state with his father in an attempt to make positive changes in his life. "It took a year and a half after my daughter was born that I realized that I needed to change my life or I would be financially unstable just paying tickets off. I didn't want to be on a downward spiral. It was always on my mind to change, I just couldn't." He largely communicates with his daughter via Facetime, photographs, and texts.

Although it's scary to believe you could be pregnant, early detection and action can allow you the time and resources to better care for yourself and baby during your pregnancy. If you're feeling any, or several, of these symptoms, taking an at-home pregnancy test could help confirm your suspicions or quell your worries entirely.

Demystifying At-Home Pregnancy Tests

At-home pregnancy tests come in two variations, digital and nondigital, and can be highly accurate if used correctly and at the right time. Timing and usage are key here—take the test too early or don't follow the directions and you might not receive an accurate reading. Most tests on the market can be found over the counter at popular drugstores, pharmacies, grocery stores, and even discount dollar stores. They will range in cost based on where you make your purchase and also what type of test you choose. Digital tests tend to cost a bit more since they have a few more bells and whistles (they'll digitally say "yes" or "no," "pregnant" or "not pregnant" for example), while nondigital tests work by showing lines, pluses, and minuses. The benefit of a digital test can be that clear "yes" or "no," "pregnant" or "not pregnant" reading. There is no deciphering if there really is a line, two lines, a plus, or minus. The test will literally tell you if you're pregnant or not. The choice is ultimately yours and based on your budget and personal taste.

At-home pregnancy tests work by measuring the amount of human chorionic gonadotropin (HCG) found in a urine sample. HCG increases with time, which means the earlier you take the test, the harder it is for the test to detect the HCG.[12] If you are very early in your pregnancy and the HCG level is below twenty-five to fifty mIU/mL, the test will be negative.[13] Although some home pregnancy tests claim to be extremely sensitive and able to detect HCG before a missed period, teens typically do not have regular or consistent timing for their periods and this early reading benefit could ultimately end up providing a false negative. For the most accurate results and better peace of mind, wait until after the first day of your missed period or even up to a week after you miss your period to take an at-home test.

In her video educating viewers on the best practices for at-home pregnancy tests, health director of *Parents* magazine Kara Corridan shared that false positives are pretty rare and that getting a positive is usually an indication of pregnancy.[14] If you've taken a test (or two or three) and it's come back positive, it's time to contact your health care provider and make an appointment to confirm your pregnancy. A health care provider will also be able to discuss your options with you if you are unsure about what to do and provide prenatal care if you want to continue your pregnancy.

Check Out Planned Parenthood

With more than seven hundred health centers across the country, Planned Parenthood is visited by millions of women, men, and teens for reproductive and prenatal support. Planned Parenthood health centers offer a wide range of affordable health care services. Although the services vary by location, they include the following:

- Pregnancy testing and services
- Abortion
- Birth control
- Emergency contraception (morning after pill)
- General health care
- HIV testing
- LGBT services
- Men's health care
- STD testing, treatment, and vaccines
- Women's health care

If you can't afford a pregnancy test or need to confirm your results, make an appointment at your local Planned Parenthood. You can search for your nearest Planned Parenthood health center to find out about the services it offers at www.plannedparenthood.org/en/health-center or call 1-800-230-PLAN to speak with a nurse or doctor's representative directly.

Importance of an Adolescent Obstetric Health Care Provider

There are many factors that go into selecting a health care provider: education, specializations, personality, location, hospital affiliations, cost, and whether they are covered in your (or your parents') insurance plan. But the biggest for a teen parent is the relationship between you and your provider. Teen pregnancies are incredibly unique and require providers who not only work directly with teens on a regular basis, but also can provide the time, effort, and energy to help teens navigate their pregnancy and postpartum with baby. "Teens need people who can help develop a good plan and support. They have to have really specialized services and make certain they are surrounded by people who can really help them. Not every obstetrician has the skill set to address the social and emotional needs of pregnant teens," says Dr. Charlene Gaebler-Uhing.[15] Dr. Gaebler-Uhing, together with nurse practitioner Melissa Vukovich, leads Children's Hospital of Wisconsin's Teen Health Clinic. Dr. Gaebler-Uhing and Vukovich work with patients, their families, and their pediatricians to address the physical, emotional, and social changes and general health care issues that are unique to teens and young adults ages ten to twenty-six.

Inspirations of Two Health Care Professionals

Dr. Charlene Gaebler-Uhing is a highly respected pediatrician. She was the National Faculty Development Scholar (a highly competitive three-year jointly sponsored program sponsored by the Academic Pediatric Association and Health Resources and Services Administration) from 1997 to 2000 and listed in the 2009 and 2010 editions of *Guide to America's Top Pediatricians*. After practicing as a general pediatrician for eighteen years, in 2012 she learned there was a critical shortage of adolescent medicine specialists and entered the adolescent medicine fellowship program from the Medical College of Wisconsin to provide care to a demographic sorely in need of support: teens and young adults. She first realized her passion for helping teens and young adults as well as talking about and preventing unintended pregnancies, while working on the West Side of Chicago in 1993. After completing her residency in pediatrics at the University of Illinois in 1991, she received a fellowship in 1993 from the University of Illinois to specialize in academic pediatrics. She taught at the teen clinic and realized quickly she wanted more for these young parents. "I want women to be able to be in control and meet their goals—regardless of what their goals are."[e]

Nurse practitioner Melissa Vukovich began working as a registered nurse specializing in reproductive health in 1997 at a Milwaukee inner-city sexually transmitted disease clinic. In 1999, after completing her master's degree as a family nurse practitioner, she was hired by Steven Matson, MD, to work for the Medical College of Wisconsin in the Department of Pediatrics' Milwaukee Adolescent Health Program. According to Vukovich, Dr. Matson was the "Father of Adolescent Medicine in Milwaukee." Dr. Matson developed clinics and programs to improve the health and future for the most disadvantaged of youth. "He had a passion for teens that was contagious and from that was born my own," she said. From there, for ten years, she operated South Division High School's Cardinal Clinic, a nearly full-service adolescent clinic in Milwaukee where she provided primary and reproductive health care to the medically underserved students and the surrounding community. "Developing relationships with kids was important. We were able to identify pregnancy risk behaviors among girls we saw requesting pregnancy tests," said Vukovich.[f] Because of this, the clinic provided counseling regarding secondary abstinence and very specific contraceptive education based on risk factors to any girl seeking a pregnancy test.

Vukovich strongly feels the need to eliminate health barriers to education. Whether seeing a teen at a school-based clinic or community-based clinic, she and her adolescent medicine colleagues use every opportunity to discuss academic achievement and adult transition. Part of their focus for understanding what motivates each patient is so they can help them develop a long-term plan and a fulfilling life. "We all fundamentally want similar things in our lives: happiness and something to look forward to in our future. High school is a place where kids can learn about setting goals, securing a job, planning for their future," said Vukovich. "If kids drop out of school because of pregnancy or other reasons, they are missing a vital piece of high school culture that prepares them for the adult world."[9] For women in particular, the lack of a high school diploma is a strong predictor of future poverty for both her and her children.

Dr. Gaebler-Uhing and nurse practitioner Melissa Vukovich shared their thoughts on several areas they see teen parents needing additional support and guidance around, such as prenatal care, how to navigate the world as a teen parent, the importance of quality child care, and the importance of a father in the lives of children.

What It Means to Be a Parent—Especially as a Mother

Dr. Gaebler-Uhing: Age does not determine your ability to mother. I've had many teen mothers who naturally are great mothers, much better than women who are ten to fifteen years older. They are loving and nurturing, putting the needs of their child before their own and their child does very well. They are eager learners about how to best care for their child and saw me, their pediatrician, as an important partner in their child's development. Many had taken a hard look at their own childhood, didn't like the way they were treated, and decided they were going to mother differently than their own mother. They actively worked to parent differently. They attended parenting classes or read parenting books and frequently had to defend to their mothers why they parented differently. These mothers realize they can't parent alone, and they developed a good support network of family and/or friends they can count on for help.

If you find yourself struggling to care for your child, look to your pediatrician for help. Be honest with your pediatrician about what is preventing you from being able to care for your child: depression, addiction, or lack of financial resources. They should be able to connect you to the resources you need.[16]

Vukovich: Parenting starts when your baby is still in the womb! Everything you do while you are pregnant affects your baby, so it's important to not put off parenting until the baby is born. I always tell my teen mothers that nutrition is very important when she is pregnant. Just like a baby needs to have a bottle or breast milk on a regular basis, a fetus needs to eat on a regular basis, too. We would never think of skipping meals for a baby or child, but teen moms often will skip meals, in particular breakfast. Pregnant woman need to remember when they don't eat, their baby doesn't eat. Drinking enough water and getting three meals a day with some healthy snacks is very important to a developing baby. A pregnant woman should also take her prenatal vitamin once a day. I generally recommend taking it in the evening or before bed with a light snack to avoid nausea. Ideally, prenatal vitamins should be started before a woman gets pregnant. It's important that pregnant teens know that the prenatal vitamins not only are a nutritional supplement but they also help to prevent certain birth defects, taking these in the first three months of pregnancy is very important. I recommend all pregnant women to talk to their OB-GYN [obstetrician-gynecologist] or midwife about any morning sickness that is interfering with good nutrition. Most morning sickness will go away after the first three months of pregnancy.

Likewise, babies need to get lots of sleep when they are born and a pregnant mom needs to be sure she is getting enough sleep to allow her body the energy to do the amazing job it is doing, creating a life! Pregnant teens should continue to enjoy time with their friends and find time to relax. They should try to avoid stress as well. Just as it would be once the baby is born, the father can play a key role in supporting the mother with nutrition, rest, stress management, and entertainment during her pregnancy. Practicing those team dynamics during pregnancy will likely prove to be worthwhile once the pace of life quickens upon the baby's arrival.[17]

What It Means to Be a Parent—Especially as a Father

Dr. Gaebler-Uhing: It is important for teen fathers to realize they are just as important as mothers. They need to make certain they are involved in their child's life. I have seen all sorts of involvement. Fathers who come to every appointment with the mother, fathers who bring their kids without the mothers, fathers who never come but are involved, and fathers who, by report, are not involved. It is great when they become involved in their child's care and come to doctor visits with the mother. Even better is when a father really steps up and brings their child in alone because he was free and the mother needed to be at school or work.

Before the baby is born, the mother and father should discuss how they will co-parent and share child care responsibilities. Like mothers, fathers need to think about what type of father they want to be to their child. And if they didn't have a good role model, they should attend parenting classes, read on child development, and become involved in a fatherhood group. Unfortunately many times fathers are involved and gradually become less involved after the mother and he split up. The children I've seen this happen to really miss their dads. So I would encourage all teen dads to take advantage of a fatherhood group. Larger cities now have organizations that focus on helping teen and young adult fathers develop the skills they need to maintain long-term relationships with their children even if he and the mother split up.[18]

Vukovich: Children truly benefit from being raised by two parents. Our health care system often fails to engage teen fathers in the care of the baby. They can be overlooked because many teen parents are unmarried or because of stereotypes of teen fathers as being uninvolved. Likewise, males of all ages are often less experienced with child care than women because many young girls had babysitting jobs prior to parenting. I think the earlier a father becomes involved in the care of the child, the more comfortable he will be with parenting, especially the care of a newborn. Caring for a newborn can be very intimidating and takes patience. Many hospitals host prenatal and parenting classes for teen parents. I recommended parents of all ages take advantage of any and all opportunities to succeed at parenting. It is a lifelong learning adventure![19]

What to Think about While Pregnant

Dr. Gaebler-Uhing: Teens should work to prepare themselves for becoming a mother. Read and learn about infant care and parenting skills; who will they rely on for help?

Also, think about child care. Who will care for the child when they return to school? You should be confident your child is safe and well cared for by your day care provider. There is a spectrum of child care available, so look for the highest quality child care within your price range from in-home, family, and child care centers. If using a family-run day care, if possible use a licensed provider. Make certain you know how many children are cared for, their ages, and the number of adults to children. In a day care center, the infant room usually has two adults to six infants. Family day cares generally have six children, but fewer if infants are in the home. Also you should know how they handle a medical emergency. Make certain they sleep infants on their backs and have CPR training. You should be able to visit and observe the child care setting before you place your child; once your child is in day care you should be able to drop in unannounced. Make certain they interact and stimulate your child; don't use the TV as a sitter. Ask how children are disciplined. I once knew a child care provider who routinely threatened her own children with a belt, which should be a red flag for anyone who was considering placing their own children in her care. Ask for references, but even if they get great references trust your intuition. If you get a bad feeling about the setting, you don't hire them. Also you will want to know if your child can attend if he or she has a cold, or what happens if you're late for pick up. If your child will attend a family-run day care, find out what the other kids are like and if any of them have behavior issues. Also make a child care back-up plan in case your primary day care isn't appropriate.

There are many things [you] must think about. Most important is [your] health care and [your] child's health care. You will need to find out if your child will be covered on your parents' insurance or will you need to get insurance through the state. You want to find a pediatrician before the baby is born. Many mothers do not realize you can make an appointment before the baby is born to see if you like a pediatrician and their practice. The mother also has to learn if she is covered on her parents' plan. If she isn't most states give pregnant individuals health care. Do teens understand what's covered and not covered on their plan?

Teen mothers should also think about if they will list the father on the birth certificate and what procedure must be followed to get the father listed on the birth certificate. Other questions to consider are Will they breast or bottle feed, or do a combination of both? Is their home a safe environment for the baby? Do they have a safe place for the baby to sleep? Do they have an appropriate infant car seat? They should think about if there are smokers in their home, since smoke exposure places a baby at increased risk for Sudden Infant Death. Are the smokers in the house willing to stop smoking or at least willing to smoke outside for the first year of the baby's life? Do they need help stopping?[20]

Vukovich: Interview child care providers, if possible before the baby is born, when you are not yet sleep deprived! Ask child care providers if they maintain a list of authorized people to whom they would only release your child if you were running late or unable to pick up your child. It's important that you feel secure in your choice of child care. Find out what their communication plan is if your child becomes sick while at day care. What time frame do you have to come pick up your child if he or she develops a fever, rash, or stomach flu? You will need to have a backup plan for child care in the event your child becomes sick and you are at school or work and for that reason make sure it is located in a convenient location. While you are there, look around; does it look clean? Are there age-appropriate toys for the children to play with or are there tiny toys in the toddler area that are a choking hazard? The more day care centers you visit, the more you will identify the pattern of safe nurturing environments and the easier it will be to detect an unsafe environment. Remember, the best thing you can do for your baby is ask questions![21]

Advice for Finishing School

Dr. Gaebler-Uhing: Since the type job you get is related to how much education you get, teens should think about the kind of life they want to provide to their child. They need to see education as an investment in themselves and their child's future.[22]

Vukovich: One of the greatest disadvantages for the mothers affected by teen pregnancy is that many drop out of high school or put off college or completing their GED. They plan on doing it after they have the baby or when the baby is one. Many say they are going to do it tomorrow and then tomorrow never happens. Getting an education is one of the greatest gifts they can give to themselves and their children. I cannot underscore that enough. Continuing their education will add tremendously to their self-esteem and sense of confidence. Whether they need to earn a living, come from poverty or wealth, or have just won the lottery, my advice for young women will always be to become educated, however they choose to do so. A woman can lose her job, her money, or her partner. However, she will never lose her education or the knowledge, pride, and confidence she gained from the experience. There is a strong element of strength and resiliency that is sewn through the fabric of a woman's life when she has the experience of an education to call her own, and the benefits of this will truly resonate through the lives of her children.

The sage advice to young mothers from those of us who have raised children is that their sleeping baby won't miss them as much as an older child, so they should take advantage of the baby's first year of life to finish high school or get their first year of college in. It will only get harder to finish school when kids are toddling around and having separation anxiety, and even harder yet in the preschool years when they have given up nap times. As the years go on it seems they still need you but in different ways, but they recognize your absence more. So the time for you to go to school in most cases is now![23]

What All Children Need

Dr. Gaebler-Uhing: You do not need to have lots of money to give the most important thing your child needs: unconditional love. Kids do well if they feel well cared for and supported.

Babies' brains grow and develop better if they hear lots of words and get lots of positive attention from their parents. Studies show children who do better in school have heard four times as many words by two years old than those who don't. These children also were found to be more likely praised for positive behaviors. So moms and dads should talk, read, and sing to their newborns and infants all the time. Talk to them as you change their diaper, feed them, and dress them. You need to catch them in the act of doing good behaviors. If you find your child only getting your attention when they are doing something bad, you need to figure out how you can be more present with them.

Discipline comes from the word *disciple*, which means to teach, not to punish. Punishment should only be a small part of your discipline. Before the age of three, behavior modification is how you shape your child's behavior. Reward the behaviors you want, ignore those you don't. Many of the important behaviors you will want your child to have as an adult: kindness, honesty, and cleanliness are learned through role modeling your behaviors. Your pediatrician can help you learn the best method to use according to your child's age and development.

During the first nine months of life you can't spoil a child. You shouldn't let them cry it out. Newborns should be picked up as soon as possible; the baby either needs to be fed, changed, or comforted. Taking care of their needs is how they learn to trust you. The ability to trust their mother is important for how they will function the rest of their life! Aggressive behaviors later in life have been linked to babies not having their needs met and not getting enough attention during the first two years of life. So give you baby lots of attention![24]

Vukovich: Experienced parents know that babies don't come with an instruction manual, but wish they did! As new parents, it's ok to ask questions, and health care providers consider it healthy to ask questions. One of the best things new parents can do is educate yourselves with whatever stage of life your child is at and identify experienced parents around you with well-behaved children who you respect and can ask advice. Books I read while raising my own children and recommend to my patients, friends and family are

- *Caring for Your Baby and Child: Birth to 5 Years* (2009) by the American Academy of Pediatrics.
- *Secrets of the Baby Whisperer: How to Calm, Connect, and Communicate with Your Baby* (2005) by Tracy Hogg, for the first year to help with sleep issues.
- *Secrets of the Baby Whisperer for Toddlers* (2003) by Tracy Hogg and Melinda Blau; helps with sleep issues and terrible twos.
- *1–2–3 Magic: Effective Discipline for Children 2–12* (2010) by Thomas W. Phelan, PhD; helps with discipline and preventing the need to yell at your kids.

Just when I felt like I was in a rut or feeling frustrated I knew it was time to reach out to some parents and find another book to read. In doing so you will find you are not alone and will quickly get back on track. However, the most important part of reading any of these "manuals" is that the baby's father and any caretakers (i.e., grandparents) also need to either read the books or get briefed on the principles, because if there is not consistent parenting, your child will be confused and you will all be frustrated.[25]

Finding the Right Doctor

Teens might not find their perfect doctor right out of the gate. "This is the art of practicing health care. Not everyone can interact effectively with a teen," says Vukovich. "You have to be comfortable as a provider. It starts with being open, honest, nonjudgmental, and not acting like a teen. You don't want to be an imposter. You want to be genuine." Vukovich's fifteen years of experience caring for adolescents has shown her the importance of teens having an obstetrician who is fluent in adolescent health and well-being. "I have provided care to a diverse population of teens, in a multitude of settings and am passionate about adolescent health care. While every child deserves the best care, teens often have unique health care needs that are not like that of a child nor an adult. It's important to have clinicians who are dedicated and skilled in caring for today's youth, because they are our future."[26]

Vukovich's experience has taught her to trust in teens' intuition and ability to read a situation. If, during a meet and greet or phone screen with a potential provider, a teen doesn't experience strong eye contact, authentic and empathetic questions, and a clear indication in the conversation that the provider cares and wants to be involved in the care of the teen and his or her child, the teen should move on to the next provider on the list. And keep interviewing until he or she identifies a provider he or she can have a long-term and strong relationship with. Teens should also feel that they have a voice and aren't being parented or talked down to. "It's not dictating what they should do, but giving them the credit to make good decisions about their health care. When a provider assists them by giving them the pros and cons—teens will make a good choice," says Vukovich.[27]

"For pediatric care, you can interview doctors. You want to go to a practice with a spectrum of providers, so you can find one that is the best fit for you," says Dr. Gaebler-Uhing.[28] Find a provider you connect with and think you can work well together. You should feel like your doctor has an appreciation of your life circumstances and can work to create a treatment plan that accommodates these circumstances.

Once you've interviewed providers and have a good understanding of your available options, it's time to make a decision and then stick to it. "Once you've

Meet and Greet Questions

You've identified a list of potential providers by doing a web search or through word-of-mouth references from your friends and family. You've cross-referenced this list to confirm all options are covered by your health care insurance plan options. Now it's time to meet and greet! Following is a list of questions to consider asking each potential provider before committing to any so that you end up with a perfect fit. Need more questions? Hop on your favorite search engine, type in "OB-GYN Interview Questions," and you'll get a ton of hits to develop a list that best fits your provider search needs.

- How long have you been practicing obstetrics and are you board certified?
- How many births have you attended?
- At what hospital will I give birth? Are there other hospitals you're affiliated with?
- What is your general philosophy of pregnancy care, including labor and birth?
- How much experience do you have with adolescent pregnancies and the unique complications/risks associated with them?
- If you're interviewing a doctor at a group practice: What are the chances of having my primary OB deliver? Do providers typically try to attend all their patients' births? If my primary OB isn't on call, can I meet with the other providers in advance?
- How much time do you allow for each prenatal visit? What do you typically cover and go over?
- What are the after-hours policies? Are you or your nurse available by phone or e-mail for questions between visits?
- How do you feel about patients having a birth plan with their personal preferences? Will you help me create a birth plan or review the one that I've written?
- Which prenatal tests do you routinely recommend?

- What kind of childbirth classes do you recommend or does the affiliated hospital provide?
- Do you perform C-sections? If not, is an obstetrician available in case I need an emergency C-section?
- What will the check-in experience look like when I arrive in labor? Where do I go? Will you be there? What should I do?
- Can I eat and drink during labor? What birthing options are available to me?
- What are my pain management options during birth?
- Does the hospital limit who's in the room with me for labor and birth? What if I want my partner *and* my mother? Can my partner stay overnight with me?
- Will I be separated from my baby after the birth? If so, when, why, and for how long? Can my baby room with me if I choose this option?
- What kind of breastfeeding support can I expect?
- What resources and support do you provide post-birth for mom and baby?

After your interview, take some time to think about how you felt. Did the doctor you met with instill a sense of trust and make you feel comfortable? Was the doctor's philosophy on pregnancy and birth on the same page as yours? Was the office clean and well run? Were the nurses and support staff friendly and accommodating? Did you feel like you were being treated as an important member of a team? If your answers are resoundingly *no*, then you may want to keep looking for a provider.

made a decision about an OB provider or pediatrician, be sure to schedule an appointment early for all routine prenatal or well child visits for baby. These visits are so important. If there is significant concern about the quality of care you will receive from the provider or realistic barriers to getting to future appointments, such as transportation, then consider changing to another provider. However, do not do so until you have scheduled an appointment at a new clinic and arranged for your records to be transferred. Do not bounce around—it's not good," says Vukovich.[29] Switching providers too often could impact the balance and consistency of your overall care plan.

The countdown to baby starts from the moment of conception. Within the next nine months, teen moms and dads encounter emotions, decisions, and challenges as unplanned as the pregnancy they are facing. Luckily, there are several resources, specialists, and organizations open to helping educate and support teen parents.

Finding out you're pregnant is life changing and can be even more so for a teen. Early pregnancy detection gives you the most time to make a myriad of decisions, from choosing whether to parent, terminate the pregnancy, or explore adoption; to selecting a health care provider; to determining the best co-parenting relationship structure. Early detection also provides you with some often much-needed time to collect yourself and your thoughts in order to share with the world that you are, in fact, expecting.

Preventing Unintended Pregnancies

Teens have a significant amount of control over their sexual and re-productive health, including ensuring they do not experience a second unintended pregnancy. The time to think about contraception if you're currently pregnant? Immediately, according to Dr. Gaebler-Uhing. "It is essential to think about what method of contraception a teen will use after delivery. Each pregnant teen should have this conversation with her obstetrician before she delivers. Even if you think you are not going to have sex after delivery, most teens only stop temporarily. You should think about the spacing you would like between children. Planned Parenthood has a great program and materials around life planning. It helps mothers map out their goals and when having their next child makes sense in their life. Thinking about this information should help teens iden-tify the best contraceptive method for them. Many methods can be started right after you deliver, so talk to your obstetrician!"[h]

TELLING FAMILY AND FRIENDS

Guilt, shame, and anxiety can be crippling emotions for female and male teens as they struggle with personally accepting their pregnancy. After acceptance, the very thought of telling parents, family, and friends can be paralyzing. While many adults prepare to tell the world in creative and charming ways, most teens dread the experience of telling their parents, caregivers, partners, and friends. Some teens, like parent Thuy Yau (interview on page 42), are so afraid to share the news of their pregnancy that they don't even tell their parents or caregivers until they are in labor. This chapter provides conversation starters, interviews with teens on their experiences, and feedback from parents and caregivers to hopefully provide teens with the resources, understanding, and confidence to have a difficult but critical conversation.

Getting pregnant can give teens a false sense of confidence in handling their situation. Teens may feel like they know the best course of action and decisions to make regarding their future and the future of their unborn child, that they are fully equipped to support a baby on their own, and that they don't need adult intervention or help; so why tell anyone? Why get their parents or caretakers involved?

This line of thinking tends to not work to a teen's advantage. It can be a way to avoid a tough conversation because telling people about a teen pregnancy presents

! Hormones Make for Hot Heads

Findings from the 2008 Massachusetts Institute of Technology's Young Adult Development Project show that "triggered by hormones at puberty, teens are more aroused, and aroused more easily, whether by something that makes them happy, angry, or excited. It is not clear, for example, whether they actually argue more often with parents, but it is clear that, when they argue, they express more anger."[a]

a mighty tense situation for most. Situations we find ourselves in, due to our own choices and behaviors that aren't socially acceptable, fall outside of family or moral codes, or conflict with our own hopes and expectations for ourselves, can make us feel less than. As a general rule, we don't like knowingly engaging in tasks or activities that make us uncomfortable. So it's perfectly understandable that when confronted with the option of telling parents and caregivers about the pregnancy and then having to potentially deal with their disdain, disapproval, frustration, and even anger, it's more appealing to think you have all the answers and don't need anyone's input or opinions.

The problem is that teens are at a distinct disadvantage when it comes to cognitive reasoning and making choices based on reason and logic. As a human race, our brains don't reach full maturity until our mid-20s.[1] Yikes.

The MIT Young Adult Development Project has been exploring and capturing research about young adulthood in order to better educate those who need a deeper understanding of the teen brain, including colleges and universities, employers, parents, human service providers, and young adults themselves. The MIT site credits researchers with the following striking example to help foster understanding: "Rental car companies have it right. The brain isn't fully mature at sixteen, when we are allowed to drive, or at eighteen, when we are allowed to vote, or at twenty-one, when we are allowed to drink, but closer to twenty-five, when we are allowed to rent a car."[2] The MIT Young Adult Development Project feels this brain maturation period all teens undergo is why it may be difficult for teens to meet adult expectations and demands for managing emotions, handling risks, responding to relationships, and engaging in complex school work or employment.[3]

Not sharing the news and being open to the questions, feedback, and opinions of parents and caregivers can be self-sabotaging for many teens, as they aren't cognitively ready to understand the planning needed to bring a child into the world at such a young age. The attitude "I have it all figured out and will handle it on my own" acts as a mechanism to get around having a difficult conversation and being open to what parents and caregivers have to say.

❗ Get Ready for a Bumpy Ride

● According to the MIT Young Adult Development Project, "Teens also show a heightened desire for emotional intensity, and for the thrills, excitement, adventures, and risk-taking that are likely to generate high emotion. The ability to regulate such emotions effectively does not typically come until young adulthood, so there is often a gap of several years between the onset of the 'accelerator' and the development of effective 'brakes.'"[b]

Life is full of situations where having a difficult conversation is required. From telling a friend or sibling to give back the shirt he or she borrowed and negotiating a more deserved grade, to moving out of the house, leaving a job for a better one, and ending a long-term relationship—understanding how to start, navigate, and end a tough conversation is a useful lifelong skill to develop and hone. Even when—especially when—everything in your body screams at you to not have the conversation. "We tend to project all sorts of ugly scenarios, which may or may not occur. All of those 'what if's' add up and staying put in the current situation just seems easier. So, we make excuses and talk ourselves into believing that someday things will change and we will never have to directly address the problem at all," writes Marla Tabaka in her *Inc.com* article "Stop Avoiding Tough Conversations: 3 Ways." "Ironically, the pain and discomfort of putting these conversations off is usually worse than the dreaded discussion turns out to be," Tabaka concludes.[4]

Having a tough conversation starts with understanding your own perceptions, insecurities, and feelings about the subject. Once you are aware of where you are emotionally, you can use the following activities and skills to develop a plan for sharing the news of your pregnancy.

Fear of disapproval, parental reactions, and losing trust can cause intense feelings of anxiety for teens. Teens who have a plan and a thoughtful approach may be able to minimize the stress associated with sharing they are pregnant with family and friends.

A Mom's Story: Finding Out Her Teen Son Is Expecting

Pam's son found out his sixteen-year-old girlfriend was pregnant when he was eighteen. He was still living at home and told Pam the day before she left for vacation. When Pam heard the news, her whole world was rocked upside down, not to mention she was going to be out of state while her son and his girlfriend decided what to do.

> My initial reaction, and I admit it's obviously not rational, but in the moment of hearing news like this you are completely shocked. I wanted to jump off a bridge because the whole situation seemed just that catastrophic to me. They were too young and neither in a position to support themselves, let alone a baby. I immediately thought, who is going to support this child? What about day care? And it hit me; the burden would just fall on me. I just knew immediately that it was going to be my and the other grandmother's responsibility. I was also concerned because my son was of age and his girlfriend was underage so I worried about the legal issues on top of the trouble he was already in for other things. I felt their lives were shattered and the odds of them succeeding and getting an education were slim and that much harder.[c]

Understand Your Own Feelings and Reactions

Believing you're pregnant, then taking a test, and finally having a doctor or health care provider confirm your pregnancy can prompt a wide range of emotions, from fear about how family and friends will take the news and being scared about what the future holds, to being in awe of bringing a new life into the world and excited to become a parent. These emotions on their own can be complex, and teens may struggle more with one or another. Before telling family and friends, hitting the pause button to sit with yourself and become aware of the many feelings and emotions racking your mind and body can give you a chance to not only register the news, but also get a better idea of what decisions you might want to make intuitively before opening the door to more opinions and feedback. Giving yourself some time to reflect also helps you feel less shocked and scared about sharing the news.

"I'm about to tell my parents that my girlfriend is pregnant! I'm nervous, excited, and nervous! I spoke to a friend that works at church who is helping me tell my parents so that I'm not scared out of my mind for too long, or too much. Once I have told them, yes they'll be upset and disappointed, but that will help take off a lot of 'weight' so I can finally relax some. Even though I have a job, and my family is wealthy, doesn't mean it will be any easier for me than someone who's living in the projects. Peers' help, and family help are the two greatest things someone can have in a situation like this, so tell close friends, family, and those that you trust. You WILL eventually have to tell your parents so get it over with, and have another family member or your gf/bf there to support you, and you'll make it through!"—CJ[d]

Make a List

The baby's father, parents, aunts, uncles, sisters, brothers, grandparents, school administration, teachers, friends, and employers will need to hear about your pregnancy at some point before you have the baby. However, telling your best friend may feel way easier than telling your mom or dad. One way to get a handle

Sex Can Shock

According to an article on TeenHealth.com, even the most progressive of parents can be rocked to the core finding out their little angel is engaging in sexual activities. "It's one thing if your parents realize you're having sex and they're OK with that. But it's another thing if they've forbidden you to date or if having premarital sex is completely against their values and beliefs. Most parents fall somewhere in the middle. For example, some parents have pretty liberal values but they're still shocked to learn their teen had sex. Even parents who know their teens are having sex can still be disappointed or worried about their future."[e]

on breaking the news and feeling more confident is to first create a list of all the people you need to talk to, and organize your list from hardest to easiest. Then, think about the outcome of each conversation a bit. Telling your BFF might be the easiest first person, but what if your BFF tells his or her parents and they call yours? Breaking the news then might be a tad more difficult. So put some serious thought into whom you tell first and know that even though breaking the news to the hardest people on your list first might cause you some discomfort, you've taken a huge first step in approaching the situation maturely and with a sense of responsibility. And remember, as Families.com writes in its article "Let's Talk about Teenage Pregnancy—Breaking the Big News," it's not easy for any teen to tell his or her parents or those people on his or her list deemed the hardest to tell: "Okay let's be perfectly real here—finding out you're pregnant while single and still living with your parents is never a picnic. There are just as few parents of teens out there that will be instantly transformed into grandparents as there are teens out there that will instantly become super parents."[5]

Tough Questions to Prep for a Tough Convo

Sometimes the best conversations are those for which we prepare. But how does one prepare? By taking the time to reflect on what you'd like to say and the challenges you foresee with the upcoming conversations—like if someone is going to be difficult or judgmental—you can practice your responses and reduce the likelihood you'll get defensive and emotional during the conversation. You may even be more open-minded and willing to hear difficult feedback. Here are some questions designed to help you understand your thoughts, emotions, and expectations for the conversation.

- What would be the best outcome or response from the person you're telling?
- What assumptions are you making about the person you're going to tell and his or her potential reaction? Are those assumptions fair based on your past relationship with this person or are you maybe really just scared and letting fear cloud your perspective?
- What makes you really mad in a conversation? Are there any phrases, body language, or other hot buttons of yours that if pressed may ignite a defensive reaction in yourself? Thinking about this ahead of time can help you better navigate your own emotions and reactions and not let those negatively impact your conversation.
- What is your biggest fear in sharing the news? What is the worst possible response you could receive? What would you do if the worst thing happened? Sometimes the "worst" is something manageable, and knowing in

Decide If You Should Go Alone or Not

Sometimes having a close family friend, beloved relative, respected member of your church or school community, or the father/mother of your child present when sharing the news can create a buffer of sorts and mini- mize the shock, anger, and sadness that often accompany a parent or caregiver's initial reaction.

advance can help quell fears and keep a tough conversation on the tracks instead of getting off the rails.

Make Some Notes and Practice

Using the questions on page 38 or prompts of your own, get out a pen or pencil and some paper or your laptop and take some time to jot down what you plan on saying. When planning, know that you can't resolve or avoid the fact the person or people you may be telling (your audience) may be quite upset by the news. Start by simply listing what you need to cover in the conversation using one to two words for each element: how you feel, the problem or issue you want to discuss, the reason or how it happened (while this might seem obvious, some parents may be shocked to hear that you're sexually active), what your plans are, and then a blank space for how they feel. After you have the initial draft of your side of the conversation, go back over your words and try to flesh them out a bit by creating full sentences. Try to stay away from sarcasm, blame, or closed-minded phrases like "I know you're mad," or "You always . . . ," or "You never . . . ," or "I can do this on my own." Use this activity to organize your thoughts and then use a mirror or a close friend to practice sharing the news. Writing down your thoughts and then practicing can help you better understand the situation you're in and then give you some emotional distance from the topic in order to better help your audience process, understand, and support the news.

Timing Is Everything

Calling your parents at work, texting them, or sharing the news when they have friends or other family members over may create more havoc than necessary.

Get the Party ... er ... Conversation Started!

The following convo-starting prompts are taken from Judy Ringer's article "We Have to Talk: A Step-by-Step Checklist for Difficult Conversations." Judy is a conflict and communication skills trainer, black belt in Aikido, and founder of Power & Presence Training and Portsmouth Aikido. Judy's advice to people nervous about starting a tough convo? "You have more power than you think." Some of her ideas may be best after you break the news, but use these ideas to think about ways in which you may kick off sharing your news:

- I'd like to talk about _____ with you, but first I'd like to get your point of view.
- I need your help with what just happened. Do you have a few minutes to talk?
- I need your help with something. Can we talk about it (soon)? If the person says, "Sure, let me get back to you," follow up with him or her.
- I have something I'd like to discuss with you that I think will help us work together more effectively.
- I think we have different perceptions about _____. I'd like to hear your thinking on this.
- I'd like to talk about _____. I think we may have different ideas about how to _____.
- I'd like to see if we might reach a better understanding about _____. I really want to hear your feelings about this and share my perspective as well.[f]

Make sure you have complete privacy when telling parents or caregivers and do so in a forum that is safe and where you can give each other your full attention.

Put on Their Shoes

Sometimes, to best understand where someone is coming from and why he or she may be having a certain reaction, we have to put ourselves in his or her shoes.

Most Parents Really *Do* Want What's Best for You

● Speaker and award-winning author Mardie Caldwell wants teens to remember that most parents aren't out to get them or make their lives miserable. "There are times when your parents may not be the easiest people in the world to talk with, and it is even worse if the subject of the conversation is something that you know will be upsetting. Remember, your parents will very likely be pretty upset by this news; they love you very deeply and they probably had dreams for you that a teen pregnancy would likely put an end to. All parents want their children to be successful and happy and having a child at a young age tends to make achieving success a much more difficult accomplishment."[9]

We have to get out of our own worldviews and imagine ourselves sitting in his or her spot. This can be an incredible eye-opener for teens as they seek to understand why their parents or loved ones might be angry, upset, or frustrated and not as supportive as they initially hoped and expected. In his book *The 7 Habits of Highly Effective People* (1989), Stephen R. Covey writes about seeking first to understand and—only once you know where the other person is coming from, how they are feeling, and what's going on in their heads—then seeking to be understood. He writes,

> If you're like most people, you probably seek first to be understood; you want to get your point across. And in doing so, you may ignore the other person completely, pretend that you're listening, selectively hear only certain parts of the conversation or attentively focus on only the words being said, but miss the meaning entirely. So why does this happen? Because most people listen with the intent to reply, not to understand. You listen to yourself as you prepare in your mind what you are going to say, the questions you are going to ask, etc. . . . And consequently, you decide prematurely what the other person means before he/she finishes communicating.[6]

It's incredibly important to make sure that you go into the conversation not with the mind-set, "I'm going to share my news and get outta there because I got this," but that you take a few deep breaths and walk into the room with the goal of truly hearing the other person. Give him or her the time and space to freak out and share his or her anger or sadness. Even if what he or she says isn't aligned with what you want to do or how you feel, that's okay. You're responsible for your own feelings and thoughts and you don't have to allow your thoughts or feelings to change. All you have to do is listen. You can't change how people feel upon hearing you're expecting, and you aren't responsible for their feelings or emotions. What you are responsible for is your own reactions and behaviors. Try not to judge their reactions, change how they feel, or get defensive at their responses. It's not easy, which is why writing down what you want to say and practicing in advance can really make a positive difference in your conversations.

Customize Your Message

How, what, and when you tell your parents, siblings, and other family members may be different than how, what, and when you tell friends, teachers, employers, and other people in your social network. If you feel certain people are going to be upset and angry, perhaps personalize the conversation by acknowledging their feelings and being honest that this news may make them mad or sad. Also, consider how far along you are when getting ready to share your news. FitPregnancy.com cites the most common reason women wait to share the news of their pregnancy early on, before twelve weeks, is due to the higher probability of miscarriage and the desire to mitigate unwanted opinions. "The thinking is that if you tell your friends and family before twelve weeks, and experience a tragic miscarriage, then you need to share that news, too. Many women believe it's just easier to keep the news to themselves than to share their sadness with others."[7]

If you've created your list of people to tell, that makes tailoring your message a little easier. You can learn from each conversation and then tweak your message a bit to accommodate the many different people in your life and the different roles you may play as you tell others. For example, what you share with your immediate family could include more details than what you're willing to share with those outside your immediate circle, like friends, teachers, and employers. Your

Simple Conversation Starters

Linda Sapadin, PhD, and author of *Now I Get It! Totally Sensational Advice for Living and Loving* (2006), wrote that if you're stumped on how to get a tough conversations started to try these simple phrases and prompts: "I don't know how to say this, but I must tell you something" or "I don't want to scare you, but there's something you need to know."[h]

immediate family may know every detail of your plans (or your uncertainty with plans), but those outside your circle may not know what trimester you're in or if you're unsure about what decision you're going to make regarding parenting, adoption, or terminating the pregnancy.

Above All, Have Empathy

When we're angry, sad, or frustrated, at our very core we want to know that the person, or people, we're talking to hears us, understands us, and is listening. This is a crucial element of having any conversation, but especially a difficult one. If the person you're talking to is crying, yelling, or getting visibly upset, use his or her reaction as a cue to ask yourself, "What would make me feel better if I felt that way?" It could be giving the person some space, or at least asking if he or she needs a minute or two alone. It could be offering to get him or her something to drink or a tissue. It could also be acknowledging that you do hear the person and are listening to what he or she is saying and how he or she feels by using the following prompts and phrases: "I hear you," "I'm listening." You could also try out what Sapadin suggests saying: "I can understand that you're angry with me

Although sharing the news is not going to be easy, teens should never subject themselves to violent or unsafe situations. If at any time in a conversation teens feel their safety—whether physical or emotional—is being threatened, they should immediately remove themselves from the environment.

because I disappointed you, and that was not the way I wanted it to work out, either."[8] The goal is to try and put yourself in the other person's shoes and give him or her some space and time to react to your news. Keep in mind, too, what therapist Drew Coster suggests—that despite receiving negative responses from some people, there are many, many people who will want to help, support, and be there for you. "In a time like this you might be surprised at how well your parents take your news, and how much they care about you. On the other hand, not all parents will be supportive. If you find yourself in a bad place after telling your parents, don't think you have to do this on your own. There is a lot of support from professionals out there, so don't think you have to rush to make a decision."[9]

In Her Words: Q&A with Thuy Yau

Thuy Yau is a freelance writer and blogger for the *Huffington Post UK* and author of the e-book *How 5 Experiences Turned My Life Around*. She also became pregnant as a teenager. In the following section, she shares her story about being a teen parent and how she broke the news to her parents. In hopes of inspiring other young parents, she offers her perspectives in a Q&A as to how she grew from the experience of being a young parent.

Author Jessica Akin (JA): Guilt, shame, and anxiety can be crippling emotions for female and male teens as they struggle with personally accepting the pregnancy. Telling parents, family, and friends can be paralyzing. What was your experience like? What were your friends' experiences like? What was your experience finding out you were pregnant? How did the father take the news?

Thuy Yau (TY): When our families first found out about our baby, the reactions weren't incredibly supportive. My mother called me stupid. She said, "How stupid could you be not to know you were pregnant?" This crushed my soul, because little did she know—I did know I was pregnant. I was just too afraid to tell her.

I lost friends because they didn't understand my new life. They thought I had ruined my life. They laughed at me. They couldn't understand why I would want to stay at home and take care of my child. Every friendship that I thought had meaning turned to nothing afterwards. But looking back as a twenty-six-year-old now, I'm glad those friendships ended. I understand now that true friends are understanding and supportive. They don't judge.

Although I lost out on experiencing nine months to shop for a cot, to look for a pram, to buy baby clothes—I am very grateful to know, now more than ever, how absolutely fortunate I am to have my husband. Lawrence has always been a great father to our three children. He's changed nappies. He's burped our babies. He's ran out to the shops just because I was craving a specific type of ice-cream whilst pregnant. He's been absolutely amazing.

People who truly know us understand that we're not like people our own age. Even when we first met at seventeen and he was eighteen, we were talking about the future. We were talking about babies and marriage. We may not have planned our first child, but she gave us the life that we had wanted all along.

Now I'm twenty-six and he's twenty-seven and we've been married for almost seven years. He still says "I love you" at the end of every text message. He still says "You look beautiful" even though I've just woken up. Our marriage works because it's based on mutual love and respect for each other.

By going through the challenges that we have, we have grown as people and as a couple. It's only made our relationship stronger.[i]

JA: Pregnancy is a complicated process and many teens experience pregnancy symptoms shortly after ovulation while others notice symptoms once they miss their period. Symptoms such as changes in appetite, weight gain, nausea, and cramping could easily be missed, or could easily be the result of something other than a pregnancy. How did you know you were pregnant? What did you do to confirm the pregnancy? How soon after finding out did you go to the doctor? How was your pregnancy? What did you worry about? Did you go to prenatal visits?

TY: This is a very heartbreaking question for me to answer because I never had the chance to experience my first pregnancy. I lost this chance completely. My pregnancy was confirmed only forty-five minutes before I gave birth!

This wasn't because my now-husband and I didn't suspect I was pregnant but because of my upsetting circumstances at the time. I grew up in a very strict,

Asian household. I was emotionally abused, criticized, insulted. It was far from an ideal upbringing. I wasn't allowed to have a say. I was made to feel worthless and useless. At one stage, I even wondered whether I was adopted. I thought that maybe that might explain why I was mistreated.

When I was six years old, I realized I needed prescription glasses. I knew I needed to get my eyes checked but I was so afraid of my mother, I never told her until I was eleven. For five years, I stumbled around. Everything around me was blurry. I couldn't even read the teacher's writing on the blackboard. Yet nobody suspected a thing.

So, when my partner and I suspected I was pregnant, I was absolutely terrified to tell my family about my suspicions. I took a pregnancy test and it came back negative. My partner and I agreed that we would take another in two weeks—just to make sure—but I was so absolutely terrified, I never took the test again.

There were times when symptoms surfaced and we both knew the truth without seeing a doctor. But my fear overcame all rational thought. It was easy to explain away the lack of period—my periods had always been irregular.

I had just forty-five minutes to come to terms with my pregnancy. I should have spent that forty-five minutes happy—I spent it terrified that my family would disown me. I was going to be an eighteen-year-old unmarried mother. To my partner and I, this was no issue. We were committed to each other, but it was how our families would react that had us both petrified.

JA: Teen pregnancies present a series of choices and options to consider. Adoption and abortion are highly controversial and charged options with their own set of emotional and long-term consequences, but in many cases, they also offer several benefits. Even within parenting, there are obstacles and challenges to consider such as co-parenting with the father and other caregivers. What kind of feedback did you receive? How did you make your decision? Did you consider all or some options?

TY: As Lawrence and I suspected that I was pregnant, the option of abortion or anything else never crossed our mind. We were deeply committed to each other and we promised each other that if I really was pregnant—then we would keep the baby. We wanted a baby. It was our fear of our families that scared us.

JA: Among the hardest challenges of a teen pregnancy are the social issues that surround a pregnant teen and the father. Did you face any judgments, criticism, and social stigmas? What was it like going out in public pregnant and then with baby?

TY: After we had our daughter, we could feel the stigma. We were visiting our daughter one night in hospital when she threw up after a feed. The nurse who took over yelled at us, "See—you overfed her! Now she's throwing up!" She looked at us with such disgust and contempt. I cried leaving the hospital that night. I wanted so badly to be a good mother to my daughter, but it didn't feel as though others had faith in us. It's hard to believe in yourself when others around you are so quick to judge and condemn you.

JA: Many teens notice a sharp decline in the number and quality of their friend-ships pre- and post-baby. Many teen moms also go into the pregnancy with hopes of the father being an instrumental figure in their life and the baby's life. What has your experience been like? How did your friends respond? The school? Parents of your friends?

TY: My husband, Lawrence, has always been great—he's such a kind and loving person—I knew he would be the same as a father.

It seems, though, that not many of our friends had faith in our relationship. Some thought we'd gotten married "just because of the baby." Little did they know—we'd actually gotten engaged very early on in the relationship but it was our little secret until he could make the ring himself. He was an apprentice jew-eler at the time!

I'm actually very glad that I've lost contact with people. I believe that life is too short to spend time with people who make you unhappy. Sometimes you just have to do what's right for you.

As for my mother, I still see her because I love her. Although I haven't forgot-ten the pain that she's caused me, I've forgiven her. I don't want to spend my life angry. I want to be at peace. And I want my children to know their grandparents.

JA: Did you do any activities like dying or highlighting hair, tanning, playing sports, tattooing or piercing, taking prescription or over-the-counter medicines (including aspirin and laxatives), and drinking and using drugs while pregnant? Do you know other teen moms who did?

TY: No. As I already felt so scared about my family's reactions, I wanted to at least protect the health of my baby. So, I refrained from doing all that. I know one teen mum who smoked. She said that the doctors told her that the stress of not smoking is far worse for the baby, than the act itself. I feel differently on the matter, but that was her decision to make and I respect that.

JA: Did you have any complications with your pregnancy?

TY: No. On the whole, everything was okay. As I wasn't a drinker nor a smoker, there wasn't anything that could potentially harm the baby. I was a healthy weight as well.

JA: How has life been after the baby? Are you treated like a teen, like an adult, a mix? How has your life changed?

TY: Life has been fantastic. I have three children with someone who is my best friend. I have grown so much as a person—I'm more organized, I know what truly matters in life, I even eat healthier! We are treated like adults now, but that was not always the case. Our parenting has been questioned and judged—by family and strangers.

Although Lawrence and I have always been committed to each other, people have always been skeptical that our relationship would last. What we've learned, however, is that people will always judge—whether you're a young or old parent. But you can make the conscious decision to hold your head up high and be proud of who you are. You know what you've accomplished and you don't need anybody else's validation.

JA: What resources do you wish you had when you were pregnant? Did people help a lot? Did your doctor direct you to anywhere?

TY: As someone who now has three children, I think the most important thing is to look after the expectant mother's emotional and mental health. When I was pregnant with my third child, I was suffering from extreme morning sickness, depression, and anxiety. I was too scared to tell anyone besides my husband. I would often cry myself to sleep. I felt really alone.

I think that expectant mothers need lots of support. They need doctors and nurses who genuinely care about their well-being. Medical experts that will look beyond the health of the baby and deeper at how the expectant parents are really feeling.

At the end of the day, we need happy parents in order to raise happy children. We can't give children the best start in life, if we don't support the parents as well.

JA: What have you learned from being a young mom? What advice would you give other young moms?

TY: I have learned so many valuable life lessons. The most important—that life may not always happen as planned, but it always works out for the best. Although my now-husband and I didn't plan to have our first so young, it was always what we wanted. We're so glad that we settled down early. Financially, we may be at a disadvantage, but we don't regret a thing. We love our three girls and we love our life as a family.

The advice I would give other young moms would be—don't lose yourself. Don't believe that your life is over. Don't give up on your career, on your hobbies, on the things and the people who matter to you.

I know that it's easy for me to say this coming from a much more positive experience, but I want other young moms to know that there is hope. So much hope. You are raising a human being—a beautiful, little child—who is going to grow up respecting you for being there. Respecting you for looking out for them, for raising them, for trying your best to give them the best start in life.

If you're feeling scared, anxious, overwhelmed—know that people want to help you. People want to support you throughout this time. You're not alone.

JA: Any questions I didn't ask, but should in order to better help teens navigate and grow from being young parents?

TY: "What were your biggest fears before you became a parent and/or when you were a new parent? Have they changed at all?"

When I was a new mother, I lacked so much confidence. I second guessed myself. I let others walk all over me and do what they thought was "right" for my child. Then I realized that I had to believe in myself. If I needed help, I had to ask for it. I didn't need to feel ashamed. Too often parents struggle because they believe that parenthood needs to be all sunshine and roses. But it's not always that way. If you can look at yourself in the mirror and be proud of the person staring back, then your ability to raise your child will improve dramatically.

"What has been the most rewarding aspect of being a parent?"

Knowing that what I'm doing as a mother is making a difference. I have seen my three girls go from breastfeeds to making their own breakfast. From crawling at home to running in their school sports carnival. From babbling to saying, "I love you, Mummy." And when I see how far they've come, I remind myself that it's because of me. That being at home for the past eight years has been so very worth it.

All parents—mothers and fathers, young and old alike—aren't paid for what they do. At least, not in a monetary sense. But the rewards come in the form of smiles, hugs, kisses, and the beautiful, unforgettable moments that make you think, "I love being a parent."

Get More from Thuy Yau

For more insight from Thuy Yau, check out her blog, *Inside a Mother's Mind*, at www.insideamothersmind.com. Her blog once focused purely on her life as a mother, but is now about personal development. She's a regular contributor to many different websites, one of which is Lifehack. If you'd like to find out why she believes being a young parent can be a very positive experience, check out her article on Lifehack.[j]

A positive result could mean teens need to learn new communication skills in order to listen to their loved ones' concerns and be able to understand and articulate how they personally feel about their unplanned pregnancy.

Telling family and friends may not be easy. You may be wrought with feelings of sadness, fear, and insecurities about the future. Understanding how you're feeling, making a plan to share the news, and then being open to what others have to say, their feelings, and even their insecurities could help give teens perspective on the next decisions to make. Showing that you care about their role in your pregnancy could also get others on your team, and you may find yourself surrounded by a wonderful support system.

THE CHOICES AHEAD: TERMINATING THE PREGNANCY, ADOPTION, AND PARENTING

According to Dr. Charlene Gaebler-Uhing, obstetrician at Children's Hospital of Wisconsin's Teen Health Clinic, there are no perfect choices for teens who are struggling with an unintended pregnancy and what to do next.

You can have an abortion, you can have the pregnancy and give the child up for adoption, you can become a single parent, or have a young marriage. There is no one correct choice; each has its unique risks and benefits. A young woman needs to look at her own life and decide which is best for her. The first two choices free you up from teen parenting, but one may later regret not having had the child. The latter two choices put you at risk for not achieving your long-term goals and lowering your lifetime earning potential, but provide you with opportunity to experience the rewards of

"At that time I wasn't with my boyfriend, but I told him we needed to talk. So I went to his house and I told him. He hugged me and started crying, he told me he was sorry for everything but that he was going to help me. After we went to go tell my parents they told me they kinda already knew it. They told me I had their support."—Isabel, who was fourteen when she got pregnant and fifteen when she had her daughter[a]

There are no easy choices when it comes to deciding whether to terminate an unplanned pregnancy, move forward with an adoption, or parent. Researching their options, talking to professionals, and finding a community of individuals in their similar situation can help teens understand their choices and then make a decision they can live with.

parenthood. It's not that one cannot achieve his or her educational goals, but one needs to be realistic that being a teen parent will make it more difficult. Data shows teen parents have very high rates of not finishing high school or obtaining a GED.[1]

Teen pregnancies present a series of choices and options to consider. Adoption and abortion are highly controversial and charged options with their own set of emotional and long-term consequences, but in many cases, they can also offer several benefits for the long-term success of the teen mom and dad. However, even within parenting, there are obstacles and challenges to consider, such as single parenting or co-parenting with the father and other caregivers. To make matters harder, teens may be receiving feedback from their parents, friends, family, and religious affiliations that conflicts with their own emotions or desires. This chapter in no way promotes any one choice over another, but simply provides data, actual stories, and perspectives on each choice. The responsibility of making and living with whatever decision is made rests solely with the teen parents. Knowing the options available and the potential benefits and difficulties of each can help teens make the best decision for themselves.

"When I got home I was brave enough to tell my parents. They were both watching TV on the lounge. I walked in and just told them straight out. They were so surprised (I was a straight A student that was in dance groups, choir, musicals, social justice group, and tennis) they never thought I would get pregnant. The first thing my mum did was hug me. My dad just kept saying you should have been more careful. After that we just talked . . . I was keeping the baby."—anonymous teen mom who was fifteen when she found out she was pregnant with twins and delivered at sixteen (although her boyfriend initially walked away from the situation, they did work things out and eventually got married, she went to college, and they later had another child).[b]

Pregnancy Termination

Sarah Grey is a women's rights advocate, writer, and editor and wrote the following about her stance on terminating a pregnancy and allowing those who choose this path an open voice and floor to talk about their decision:

And whether or not we disclose our abortions, whether or not we've even had them, let's talk as though having an abortion is a perfectly okay option

Feel Lost? Can't Make a Decision? Don't Know What to Do?

Call the Backline's Talkline at 1-888-493-0092. Backline's Talkline offers a free and confidential space to talk about pregnancy, parenting, abortion, and adoption. They offer judgment-free support at any point before, during, and after your experience, no matter which options you are considering, what decisions you have already made, or how you are feeling about it all. Counselors are available Monday to Thursday from 5 p.m. to 10 p.m. and Friday to Saturday from 10 a.m. to 3 p.m.[c]

to consider when you're very unhappy about being pregnant. Let's act like women have a choice. Let's tell our friends that there is nothing wrong with ending an unwanted, life-disrupting, economically catastrophic pregnancy, and let's listen to what they say and support them in whatever decisions they make. Let's put a human face on abortion; disagree with it if you like, but know that women you like and respect have made a different decision and have lived happily with that decision.[2]

Feel alone even thinking about bringing up abortion as a consideration? You're not. Abortion isn't easy to talk about—it ranks among the most controversial conversation topics and it is up there with terrorism, the death penalty, and same-sex marriage.[3]

Who's Having Abortions?

Half of pregnancies among American women are unintended, and four in ten of these are terminated by abortion.[4] That translates to 21 percent of all pregnancies (excluding miscarriages) ending in abortion.[5]

Abortion isn't really even a teen issue either. Only 18 percent of U.S. women obtaining abortions are teenagers and those aged fifteen to seventeen obtain a fraction of that amount, 6 percent of all abortions; eighteen- to nineteen-year-olds obtain 11 percent; and teens younger than fifteen? Well, teens younger than fifteen come in at a miniscule 0.4 percent. The biggest demographic of women obtaining abortions is actually women in their twenties and they receive more than half of all abortions: Women aged twenty to twenty-four obtain 33 percent of all abortions, and women aged twenty-five to twenty-nine obtain 24 percent.[6]

Breaking the Silence

Want to hear from other women who have been in the same situation as you? Check out the Abortion Diary at http://theabortiondiarypodcast. com. The Abortion Diary is the only publically accessible audio collection of stories from people speaking out against the shame, stigma, secrecy, and isolation surrounding abortion through sharing and reading personal stories.

> ## Abortion Defined
>
> • abortion [uh-bawr-shuh n]: the removal of an embryo or fetus from the uterus in order to end a pregnancy.[d]

Women receiving abortions, contrary to some media and religious groups, aren't godless, immoral individuals. Almost 70 percent have strong ties to their faith: 37 percent of women obtaining abortions identify as Protestant and 28 percent identify as Catholic.[7]

Women aren't having abortions because they are backing away from responsibility either; they feel they are making a well-informed and mature decision with the understanding they cannot parent given their current circumstances: 75 percent of women cite concern for or responsibility to other individuals; 75 percent say they cannot afford a child; 75 percent say that having a baby would interfere with work, school, or the ability to care for dependents; and 50 percent say they do not want to be a single parent or are having problems with their husband or partner.[8]

What Does It Mean to Terminate a Pregnancy?

Abortions are medical procedures women undergo to terminate, or end, a pregnancy. There are several methods and options for the type of termination procedure, but the methods are largely based on where in the gestational cycle a woman is. The two primary and common methods to terminate a pregnancy are an early medication abortion or a surgical abortion.

> ## Costly Procedures
>
> Unfortunately, the sheer cost of having an abortion could negatively impact teens in difficult economic situations, or teens whose families cannot afford the financial costs associated with having an abortion. A medication abortion can cost, on average, up to $800 nationally. A nonhospital abortion with local anesthesia at ten weeks' gestation averages $480 nationally.[e]

Early Medication Abortion

In September 2000, the U.S. Food and Drug Administration approved mifepristone (a.k.a. the abortion pill) to be marketed in the United States as an alternative to surgical abortion. In 2001, medication abortion accounted for 23 percent of all nonhospital abortions and 36 percent of abortions before nine weeks' gestation. Early medication abortions have increased from 6 percent of all abortions in 2001 to 23 percent in 2011, even while the overall number of abortions continued to decline. Data from the CDC (Centers for Disease Control and Prevention) show abortions shifting earlier within the first trimester, likely due, in part, to the availability of medication abortion services.[9]

An option available only within the first two months of a pregnancy, mifepristone acts in a similar way to an early miscarriage. It obstructs the hormone progesterone, causing the lining of the uterus to break down and become incapable of supporting the fetus. After taking the mifepristone in a clinic or doctor's office, patients will take the second pill, misoprostol, which works by inducing cramps and emptying the uterus. According to Planned Parenthood, "More than half of women abort within four or five hours after taking the second medicine. For others, it takes longer. But most women abort within a few days."[10]

Surgical Abortion

Surgical abortions take place in a clinic and include aspiration (the most common method) and dilation and evacuation.[11] Aspiration is also known as the vacuum method or vacuum aspiration. Aspiration is usually used up to sixteen weeks after a woman's last period.[12] For those women looking for an abortion after sixteen weeks, the primary option is a dilation and evacuation, also known as a D&E.[13]

During an aspiration abortion, you will be offered something to relieve the pain and might have the option to be sedated. The health care professional will then dilate your cervix in order to stretch it and increase the size of the opening in order to insert the suction device, which is used to empty the uterus. Sometimes, an instrument called a curette is used to remove any remaining tissue that lines the uterus.

During a D&E, the initial process will be much the same in which you receive medication and sedation to ease your experience and pain.[14] In later second-trimester procedures, you may also need a shot through your abdomen to make sure that the fetus's heart stops before the procedure begins. The procedure then concludes with a suction instrument or machine gently emptying your uterus.

In Her Words: A Poem on Loss

Guy says, You know what to do.
I waited for the just joking,
the, we'll be fine, right?
Three weeks? Was it more?
All I knew was "it" remained.
"It" always unnamed.
God, what do I do?
Silence.
So, mom helped pick what's right.
I get the remains.
Pro-life's no joke.
Peaceful protestors with signs. Taunts. And more.
Protect the unnamed.
Pro-choice now a right.
My new label.
Whore.
My dad's name for it.
Slut.
And more.
No money for meds.
I did it awake.
Guess what?
Guilt stains.
No joke. [15]

Risks

Although a first-trimester abortion is one of the safest medical procedures, with minimal risk of less than 0.05 percent, teens are more likely than older women to delay having an abortion until after fifteen weeks of pregnancy, when the medical risks associated with abortion are significantly higher. Paying for the abortion could be the primary reason teens delay and they wouldn't be alone; nearly 60 percent of women who experienced a delay in obtaining an abortion cite the time it took to make arrangements and raise money. [16]

However, it's important to note that while waiting is an option, the risks increase as the pregnancy matures. Abortions performed in the first trimester pose virtually no long-term risk of such problems as infertility, ectopic pregnancy, spontaneous abortion (miscarriage), or birth defect, and little or no risk of preterm or low-birth-weight deliveries. [17]

Thinking about an Abortion?

Find out more information by speaking directly to your health care provider. If you don't feel comfortable discussing abortion options with your current provider, reach out to your local Planned Parenthood for more information on your options, the costs, what to expect during the procedure, how it feels, and care afterward. You can find a Planned Parenthood heath center near you by visiting www.plannedparenthood.org/.

Worried about the long-term psychological impact of having an abortion? Leading experts have concluded that among women who have an unplanned pregnancy, the risk of mental health problems is no greater if they have a single first-trimester abortion than if they carry the pregnancy to term.[18] This is not to imply that teens won't experience any emotional or psychological distress, but that research shows having an early abortion is on par with the level of emotional stress of having a baby.

What if a teen isn't ready to parent or doesn't have any support infrastructure? What if that same teen, while knowing he or she cannot personally parent, also has opted against an abortion? There is another option to consider: adoption.

Adoption

Adoption provides teens with the ability to place their child in the care of loving, committed families who are ready to take on the financial and daily responsibilities of parenting. Understanding the facts, benefits, and process of adoption can make it easier for a teen to make a decision regarding the long-term well-being of his or her child.

What Is Adoption?

- Adoption is the transfer of parental rights and responsibilities from one family or person to another.[f]

"Knowing that 'my kids' are being raised by a mom and dad [whose] whole world revolves around them is a great benefit; I never worry. Adoption doesn't have to be an experience to be ashamed of. I'm proud of the decision I made and the fact that 'my kids' will have opportunities I couldn't provide."—Amy, birth mother to two children[9]

Common Fears

One of the biggest fears of moving forward with adoption is the social stigma and judgments about giving your baby up. The statement "giving your baby up" is a myth and a judgment statement. As EnlightenMe.com writes in its article "What Birth Parents Should Know about Adoption," "Giving a child the best chance to live a happy, productive life isn't 'giving up'—it's heroic."[19] An adoption does require the teen to see the pregnancy to full term, and because of this, teens can face significant social and psychological pressures and difficulties. Many adoption agencies, like the American Adoption Association, can help to maximize confidentiality by helping teens purchase baggy clothing or providing a temporary out-of-town living situation.[20] Teens always have the option to maintain their own privacy and not communicate their pregnancy and decisions publically, unless they are ready and that's what they desire.

Many birth parents also worry their children will also experience academic, social, and psychological disadvantages as adoptees. But many organizations and even adoptees themselves state this isn't the case at all and that adopted children can and often do grow up well-adjusted and happy. A 1994 study conducted by the Search Institute in Minneapolis evaluated 881 adopted adolescents and their adoptive parents over four years and found the teens scored higher than their non-adopted counterparts in caring and social competency.[21]

Strong Adoptions

Although there are a myriad of fears that can arise when considering adoption, birth parents should know that many children in adoptive families do extremely well. Many individuals were so resilient because they received strong support around their transition from birth to adoptee family. Postadoption services are cited as being important and even instrumental in the well-being of the adoptee.

In Her Words: Q&A with Ann Angel, Mom of Four Adopted Children

Ann is a professor and the graduate program director at Mount Mary University in Milwaukee, Wisconsin. She is an accomplished writer, having published many books, including six in print, and received several awards: Mount Mary University Alumnae Madonna Medal in 2012, Mount Mary University Teaching Excellence Award in 2011, the American Library Association YALSA Excellence in Nonfiction Award in 2011, and the Council for Wisconsin Writers Nonfiction Award in 2010. She is also a parent of four children through adoption and with her daughter Amanda recently edited a collection of personal stories written by birth mothers, adoptive mothers, and adoptees called *Silent Embrace: Perspectives on Birth and Adoption* (2010). Amanda also has a very special story, which she shares later in this chapter, as an adoptee and birth mother.

Ann opened her heart and in the following Q&A shares her story to help teen parents understand her perspective as an adoptive mother and the impact being able to adopt has had on her, and her family's, life.

Author Jessica Akin (JA): What encouraged you to consider and then decide to adopt?

Ann Angel (AA): I'm the second oldest of nine kids and my husband Jeff is an only child. I loved being around family and he loved the way something was always going on at my house. Before we married we knew we'd have a large family and we expected to adopt some of our kids because it didn't seem right to bring a bunch of kids into a world that's struggling to sustain us all.

We didn't end up having birth children, but adoption was such an easy decision for us that I've always felt we have the family that was the family of our dreams.[h]

JA: Please share your experience with the adoption process. How did you feel going through the process? What were your worries and fears?

AA: The process of going through a home study can feel intrusive and intense because of the questions, the house visit—I recall vacuuming everything including the window sills and crevices in the steps only to have my social worker ignore all that and just take a seat in the living room. Although I recognize the entire process of investigating an adoptive home is intended to make sure we're able to raise a child and to learn more about our parenting style as well as to help us understand the ways we might handle questions about our family's origins, there were times I secretly feared I would be turned down because I wasn't good enough. But I also felt as if I was well-prepared to parent because of the way questions would come up and I would learn more and more about how I might handle difficult moments as a parent. With each adoption, more and more support services became available in our community and I became involved in writing for state newsletters. All of this made me feel a strong part of the adoption community.

JA: Were you able to develop a relationship with each birth mother? What about the birth fathers? How did you get to know the birth families and do you have any suggestion for teens in developing relationships with the adoptive family?

AA: My two oldest children were born at a time when people were only beginning to understand the value of talking openly about adoption. Those are closed adoptions. My oldest has tried to learn more about her origins and possibly meet her birth mother, but her birth mother isn't ready. Our younger son was born in Mexico and we could easily find his birth father and birth brothers, but he has no interest. Our youngest daughter had an adoption in which we exchanged letters, but we opened it when she turned eighteen. She's known her birth mother for almost ten years and wants a relationship but it's complicated. For a while she asked me to maintain communication but she just didn't feel she could. I think that adopted kids can fear they're being disloyal to the family they live with, and I think it's super important for adoptive parents to support the relationships. We've tried to get everyone together when possible. Meanwhile, our youngest daughter is slowly becoming more involved with her birth family because I believe she trusts that we'll always love her and we don't see it as disloyal.

JA: What advice do you have for teen birth mothers who aren't sure of the type of adoption or relationship they desire with the adoptive family? What have you found are important things to consider when deciding on the adoption structure?

AA: I think birth parents need to keep adoptive parents informed about medical issues even if they choose closed adoption or an adoption in which there's minimal contact. The decision to create an open or partially open adoption is going to be one that should be carefully considered and discussed with adoptive parents. I also think everyone involved in adoption should be prepared to listen to the child and include the child in decisions about visits as the child gets older. The most important thing I've learned about adoption structures is that all the parents can make a plan and stick to it, but life circumstances and an adopted child's growing independence and self-awareness will change that plan. It's important to communicate but to recognize that each individual is going to go through times of silence and times of emotional need. As I said, it's complicated and teen birth mothers should probably be prepared for some ups and downs emotionally and be prepared to be patient, to maintain a healthy lifestyle yourselves, and to work at relationships.

In some cases, birth mothers might be considering allowing an extended family member to adopt the baby. In this case, I think it's important to be sure you're comfortable with the possibility of seeing this child frequently.

JA: What struggles have you faced as an adoptive mother? Do you think there are any parenting strategies or special circumstances that are unique to adoptive families that would be good for birth families to understand?

AA: I don't know for sure how many of my struggles are typical of adoption or are just typical of parenting.

JA: Many adoptive families celebrate and honor the backstory of their children by celebrating their "Gotcha Day," educating them about or helping foster an interest in any cultural differences and helping them find their biological parents. Could you share what traditions, activities, and support you and your family provided to your children?

AA: We don't really celebrate adoption days. I, personally, wasn't comfortable with the concept because, although each day we met our children and brought them home was a joyous day for us, I also realized that another woman or couple was experiencing a loss. It doesn't feel right to me to celebrate that. Instead, as a culturally mixed family, we try to create traditions that weave a blend of cultures into our holidays and celebrations. We've celebrated the Day of the Dead more than we've celebrated Halloween, and we've honored Kwanzaa traditions. We're so lucky to live in a city where ethnic celebrations and festivals are big and we often attend these together. But there are other more subtle things—things that I hope have become engrained in our adult children's lives—that we do. This includes making diverse friends, and bringing diverse art and books and activities into our home on a regular basis and making these a part of our lives. My kids have all attended high schools that required service projects, and so I worked as the parent volunteer and connected adopted high school students to the Coalition for Children, Youth and Families (http://www.coalitionforcyf.org/), an organization that unites a variety of adoption services and provides support groups and parent training, to work with younger kids and their families on games and activities at family events. One year, the teens, all adopted from a variety of countries and cultures, helped younger kids to make handprint tiles for their families; another year, the teens helped the kids make friendship bracelets. What I loved about this is the way the teens gained insight into how young parents, and their own parents, thought about creating their families. They shared their own adoption stories and gave the younger kids opportunities to talk and think about the importance of their family bonds. These events were open to birth parents, foster parents, and adoptive parents as well as their children.

Now that my children are older I see them reaching out to pregnant teens and adopted teens to listen to their stories and to provide emotional support. Meanwhile, I've become more and more involved in work that provides educational and emotional support to teens with fewer advantages than my kids had through my work at Mount Mary University, where I teach writing.

JA: What advice and suggestions do you have for teens considering adoption as an option? Are there any books, movies, or other resources you feel could help them as they make a decision?

AA: Dear teens considering adoption as an option,

If you're thinking about adoption, you are probably aware of limitations in what you can do for your child. You probably already know that adoption is a legally binding decision, but that doesn't always mean you must drop out of your child's life completely. For this reason, you need to be involved in making an adoption plan that you're comfortable with. If you only want to exchange pictures and letters, seek adoptive parents who will agree. If you want more involvement, seek adoptive parents who are willing to make you a part of their lives and be willing to talk to them about how you will take responsibility for your own life so that you can be a positive role model for your baby. Be prepared for shifts and changes in your relationships throughout the years of your child's growth. For instance, I have a daughter who placed her baby in an open adoption. While she was pregnant, she met with the adoptive parents and told them that she would step back and allow them to parent the baby although she wanted annual photos and letters. She promised she would always respond to them if they sought her out but she didn't want to interfere in their lives as they built their family. When her birth daughter was ten, she asked to see her birth mother and, since then they visit together at least once a year. They've gone camping together and have developed a really strong extended family. This daughter was born into a closed adoption and has no contact with her birth family although she has tried to open her adoption. My two sons, both in closed adoptions, are not interested in opening their adoptions. But, then, my youngest daughter met her birth mother when she was eighteen. In each case, I think the most important thing you need to keep in mind is that, despite shifts and changes, you all need to respect one another and talk honestly about feelings and responses. But the very most important thing you can do is to make sure you know what you're choosing when you select a couple to parent your child. On those difficult days, when you're missing your baby—and you will miss your baby—please know that the adoptive parents know this was heartbreaking, even if hopeful for you, and they will do everything they can for the child you will share, even if it's a closed adoption. We adoptive parents are always so very grateful to you for giving this child life and for making sure this child was raised in the sort of family you wanted for him or her.

In making a decision about whether adoption is right for you, I think the best movie you can watch is *Juno*, which came out in 2007. There's an older film called *Immediate Family* (1989) starring Glenn Close that also follows a birth mom trying to decide who her baby's parents will be. While there are a ton of books for adoptive parents, my daughter discovered there wasn't a lot out there written specifically for birth parents and so we coedited a book, *Silent Embrace: Perspectives on Birth and Adoption* (2010). This book can provide looks into what it feels like to make the decision to open or close an adoption as well as how adopted children feel about their very complex family relationships. Many states have support organizations such as Wisconsin's Coalition for Children, Youth, and Families. You might seek them out for support groups and reading materials, or contact Wisconsin's coalition (http://www.coalitionforcyf.org/). They're a great support service for everyone involved in adoption.

JA: What do you think are the most important traits for teens to think about when choosing adoptive parents for their child?

AA: I think a teen must first consider a couple's potential ability to nurture the child. Are they a couple you believe will work together in the best interest of their children? Do you get a sense that they will love this child unconditionally? Then you'll want to consider a couple's financial stability—this doesn't mean the couple needs to be super wealthy, but you want someone who's going to be able to raise this child to readily give him or her a stable home, and a good education. You might have particular spiritual or religious or ethical views that you want your child to share so look at these elements and consider how important they are to you. If you want an open adoption, is this couple comfortable with making you a part of the extended family or only comfortable with sharing pictures, and how do you feel about a semi-open or completely open adoption? That's critical to how comfortable you're going to feel about your decision.

JA: Any final thoughts or words of wisdom for teens who find themselves in this situation?

AA: Consider your options carefully and don't rush to make a decision because you're afraid. If you can't talk to your parents about this, you might want to talk with other adults in your life about this choice. If you know someone who has placed a child for adoption, you'll be amazed to find out how willing they are to talk about their experiences and to listen to yours. My oldest daughter has made herself available to many birth parents in this way. There are birth parent support groups too. You might want to take a look at the list I found at http://www.americaadopts.com/resources/birth-mother-support-groups/.

Finally, don't let anyone talk you into something that doesn't feel right. If you are convinced that adoption is the best option, make sure to find parents who will be the very best fit for what you want for this baby.

Since many adoptees struggle with feelings, emotions, and challenges that non-adoptees may not, they can benefit from counseling, therapy, and other services geared toward helping them understand their feelings and family structure. Adoptive parents can also help their children by seeking out other adopted children in their communities to help build a network. Adopted children make up roughly 2 percent of the total child population under the age of eighteen, but 11 percent of all adolescents referred for therapy have been adopted.[22] Finding like-minded individuals can help adoptees understand and manage their unique family structure. Birth parents considering adoption can ensure their child receives the support and psychological care through the transition and their ongoing experience by stating their wishes and expectations to the adoptee family. This can further reduce fears around their child not being as successful or happy as those raised by birth parents. Understanding the types of adoption structures available and what rights birth

A Movie Must-See

Juno is a 2007 film that follows a young girl, Juno, faced with an unexpected pregnancy. Juno grapples with the decision on whether to keep the baby and then, once she decides to keep the baby, struggles with whether to move forward with adoption. With the help of supportive parents and friends, Juno starts to understand herself better, which helps her make decisions regarding the baby and her future. Produced by Fox Searchlight Pictures, Mandate Pictures, and Mr. Mudd; available online and via DVD; it runs 96 minutes.

"I thought I could give her up and forget about her, with no strings attached. It may sound sad, but it's being honest. I had to learn to accept it and deal with it. I lost the bonding between a child and parent. I gave birth to her, but I don't know her. I don't feel her pain, see her smiles, watch her take her first step, say her first word. . . . You, as a parent, must put your child's interest first. . . . Life is not perfect or fair. Every day I think of my child, but it gets easier. I watch her grow up in pictures and every day I thank the Lord that I got to bring this Angel into this world, even if it means that someone else will have the joys, heartaches, pains, and happiness of this child. I brought happiness to a couple that couldn't have that happiness unless a birth parent like me gave it to them. . . . As a birthparent I will always play the 'what if' in my head, but deep in my heart I'm happy with the choice I made."—Jody, a birth mother of one[i]

parents have can help mitigate and reduce concerns birth parents have around adoption.

Types of Adoptions

There are two primary types of adoption structures for birth parents to consider: open and closed. Both offer birth parents the ability to define the type and level of their involvement in their child's life.

Closed Adoptions

In a closed, or confidential, adoption, all paperwork is completed through a third party, allowing the birth and adoptive parents to remain anonymous to each other. The third party is usually an adoption agency, law firm, or attorney. In this type of adoption, birth parents choose to allow the adoptee family an exclusive relationship with the child and choose to physically seal the adoption papers and remain outside of the child's life until he or she turns eighteen. It's important to note that although there is no identifying information provided to the birth or adoptive family about each other (like physical and mailing addresses, names, or phone numbers), both families are often provided with information about each other's physical characteristics and medical histories to help each other make a

Adoption's Costs to Birth Parents

Although each state has specific and different laws that govern who can receive assistance and how much, birth parents typically receive full medical coverage for the pregnancy and birth and also financial assistance for rent and utilities, food, transportation, maternity clothing, and even phone services.[j]

confident decision regarding their individual families. Closed adoptions can provide a sense of peace and closure to the process, but can cause a bit more stress and longing on the side of the child who may want to better understand his or her background, family history, and even medical history as he or she gets older.

Open Adoptions

The term *open adoption* covers a wide variety of structures and preferences on behalf of both the birth and adoptive families. Open adoptions allow both the birth and adoptive parents access to each other and even control in the decision-making process of raising the child. In an open adoption, birth and adoptive parents can communicate regularly with each other, meet, and stay engaged in each other's lives and the life of the child. From simply receiving pictures and phone calls throughout the year and being invited to birthdays and milestone events, to having an active role in the parenting and daily life of the child, open adoptions can provide birth families with varying levels of involvement.

It wasn't until recently that so many adoptions were open. Most were closed, and a possible reason the trend is increasing for open adoptions is that they are being credited with helping children acclimate to being adoptees. At the same time, while this structure provides a significant amount of comfort to birth parents and can offer additional support for the child, some adoptive families struggle with insecurities and fears around open adoptions, worrying that birth parents will intrude upon their family life or decide they want to parent after the adoption is final. Adoptive families also cite fears of the child being unsure of the roles of both sets of parents. Just as adoptive families should be understanding of the birth parents' fears, birth parents should consider the concerns, fears, and worries of the potential adoptive families they are interviewing.

Although birth parents and adoptive parents alike can research the pros and cons of each arrangement until they are blue in the face, unfortunately, there is no

Agency Differences

State adoption agencies are usually of two types, public and private. Public agencies are run by the states themselves, whereas private agencies are only licensed by the states. Public agencies typically have lower costs involved in adoption, whereas private agencies can sometimes charge a great deal to the adoptive family.[k]

direct right or wrong answer. Many who have experienced closed or confidential adoptions swear by them, and the same goes for those in open adoptions. For teen parents, it will come down to being emotionally aware and knowing what type of relationship is most desired, doing adequate research to determine the benefits and contingencies of each structure, and then making a personal decision about what arrangement they are most comfortable with as birth parents.

Parenting: Issues Teen Parents Face

Because many teens will make the decision to parent, the remainder of this book is centered on the common trials, obstacles, and stigmas teen parents face. When

Need Help Understanding Your Options?

American Adoptions can help teens navigate the complex emotions and challenges of an unplanned pregnancy. From receiving insight on how to make healthy decisions for yourself and baby to building a support system, understanding your options for finishing your education to making a decision for yourself and baby, adoption specialists are available twenty-four hours a day, seven days a week to talk to teens. Simply call 1-800-236-7846 for free support and information.

In Her Words: Q&A with Amanda Angel

Amanda Angel is an elementary school teacher and together with her mom, Ann from the interview on pages 60–66, Amanda coedited a collection of personal stories written by birth mothers, adoptive mothers, and adoptees called *Silent Embrace: Perspectives on Birth and Adoption* (2010). In the following Q&A, Amanda shares her story as an adoptee and birth mother to help provide some perspectives, insight, and hope to teens struggling with an unwanted pregnancy.

Author Jessica Akin (JA): What was it like to be an adoptee? Could you share some of your favorite memories? What positive impact do you think being an adoptee has had on your life?

Amanda Angel (AA): In our family, being an adoptee was just a part of who we were. We always knew that we were adopted, in the hopes that it would never be looked at as a shameful secret. I still get a kick out of people telling me and my siblings that we look like our parents or one another! The four of us look nothing alike, although I'm sure some of our mannerisms are similar.

I can't really say what positive impact it's had other than I've had the opportunity to have a life and one that is with an incredible family. It's hard to say because I don't know any other existence other than being an adoptee.[1]

JA: Do you have a relationship with your birth family? As an adoptee and someone who has spent a lot of time counseling, researching, and working with adoption and adoptees, what do you see adoptees wishing for, or having a deep desire to know/understand, about their birth families?

AA: I reached out to my birth mom about eight years ago and although she was found, she explained to the agency that she was not interested in a relationship at that point. The impetus to search came from questions from my birth daughter's parents about health history. Prior to that, I had no real drive to search. My mom was always very supportive of seeking out our birth families, but I never felt I needed to do it. However, with another person relying on me for medical information, I decided I may as well try to meet my birth mother in addition to getting my history. I was surprised how devastated I was when I found out she did not want to have any contact. My hope is to retry this summer.

I think most people want both answers, as well as that visual connection of looking at someone's features and seeing yourself. Many adoptees also want to know why they were placed.

JA: As a birth mom, please share your experience with the adoption process. How did you feel going through the process? What were your worries and fears?

AA: My decision to place my daughter at twenty-two hinged on my circumstances at that point in my life. Knowing that keeping her would have meant raising her in an abusive environment—emotionally, mainly—I could not see any other option for her. I had made my decision very early on in my pregnancy and had the support of my family and close friends. Of course, being pregnant for the first time instills many worries and fears, which just heightened my worries about making the wrong decision for her. I was worried about whether or not I'd find the right parents for her (which I did!), worried about how I would tell people about her without shame, and worried that I might not survive it even though it was my own decision.

When you spend nine months carrying this bundle of love and knowing that you would not get to see her grow and change through daily life, it makes that decision even scarier. At the very end of the process, I had chosen her parents and they would visit with her on the weekends. One weekend I asked them to stay home in Minnesota so I could have those two days to really say my goodbyes, spending hours snuggling, singing to her, and whispering into her teensy ears my hopes and dreams for her future. They were extremely understanding, telling me through tears that they would understand if I changed my mind and kept her. Her mom even said she knew that I would be an incredible mother—better than her even—because she has watched me and could see that I was a natural.

JA: Any time we make a decision, as much as we may know it's the right one, there is always a feeling of loss. How did you manage the feelings of loss after finding, and then sharing, your daughter with her adoptive family?

AA: My loss was great, but I had time to prepare for it mentally. I did a lot of journaling and dove into work and finishing school to make sure I was too busy to think too much. Nights were hard—a lot of tears were shed into my pillows. I always had contact through letters and pictures. I saw her fourteen months old and she snuggled right into me. When she was seven, we started more frequent visits. As she has gotten older, our visits have moved from once a year to three or four. She has stayed with us for long weekends—camping or just at our house. I always told her parents that I would never initiate contact, as it was their family now, but they have always maintained contact of some sort. In fact, they drove a total of twelve hours to spend four hours at my son's first birthday party. They have also invited us to visit them this summer as well. I know I am fortunate to have the sort of relationship I have with them, as this is not the norm.

I am sure that there are still aspects of loss, but I don't know that I can pinpoint them. I don't feel like she's my daughter necessarily because I haven't raised her. However, she is someone special to me because she is, in fact, my daughter. That's a kind of odd thing to say but I don't know any other way to describe it.

JA: What role did the birth father play in your daughter's adoptive experience? What advice do you have for birth moms that do not have supportive birth fathers?

AA: In an effort to control the situation and me, he was refusing to agree to the adoption for the majority of the pregnancy. He wanted to raise her; however, at the time he was studying to be a priest. At about two months pregnant, he was harassing me and my family, so a two-year restraining order was put in place. This dictated his involvement and contact with me, so it wasn't really a cut-and-dried situation.

For those women who don't have supportive birth fathers, they need to determine if they are willing to do this on their own. It can be done, but they need to recognize that the father has rights, so they have to be ready for anything! The father could come out of nowhere at the end of the process and throw in a curveball.

JA: Have you been confronted with any negative perspectives or judgments with your decision? How have you handled and healed from outside criticism? On the flipside, have you also received a lot of support, love, and understanding?

AA: I have had some people make comments that were less than supportive. It taught me quickly that advocacy and education about the birth mother's role in adoption is lacking. I was hyperaware of the stigma—many people assume that birth mothers are promiscuous, uneducated, poor, addicts, young, and lack common sense. In fact, I had a woman ask me if I had a one-night stand and that is why I gave her away. First of all, I didn't give her away; I placed her into the arms of a loving couple. Secondly, I had been in a relationship, not a healthy one, but nonetheless a relationship of about two and a half years. I also had people comment while I was pregnant that it was wrong of me to give up my own blood. They felt it was irresponsible and an easy way out of a tough situation. I didn't even know how to respond other than saying that I had a different viewpoint since I, too, am adopted.

Of course, on the flip side, there are so many people who are supportive and loving.

JA: What advice do you have for teen birth mothers who aren't sure of the type of adoption or relationship they desire with the adoptive family? What have you found are important things to consider when deciding on the adoption structure?

AA: I found it best to voice your thoughts on what you think you would want in the future. Don't hold back and don't settle for a relationship you don't want. They need to be respectful of the decision you are making and the way they can do that is to hear your thoughts. I would say, however, if you are placing your child, then you do need to be understanding of the fact that you are no longer a central figure and respect their boundaries and limits.

For me, personally, I felt it was really important that they establish their family unit without me in the picture. When they felt they had created that, they could add me in. I told them that I would not initiate contact because I did not want to upset the balance. Over time they have welcomed my contact without them initiating it. However, that took over ten years to achieve. Even still, my contact is minimal because I want them to truly feel like a family.

JA: What do you think are the most important traits for teens to think about when choosing adoptive parents for their child? What were some of your considerations and priorities?

AA: Choosing the most important traits is really an independent process. It depends upon what the birth mother values herself.

For me, I wanted to know that the couple had been together for a while and were established financially and emotionally. I also wanted a family that was educated and smart. They didn't necessarily have to have a ton of money, as long as they were hard workers. Since my daughter's parents were considered older for starting a family, it was important to me that they had a larger extended family so that she would have cousins and aunts/uncles to lean on, if necessary.

JA: What struggles have you faced as both an adoptee and as a birth mother?

AA: I think the biggest struggle for a long time was feeling like I didn't have that blood connection. My birth daughter was the only blood connection I had and I was placing her in other people's arms. It never bothered me as much as it has more recently. My husband's family is heavily into genealogy and it always makes me think that my personal bloodline is untraceable and that bothers me, at times.

Now, having my son, I feel like I get to see myself in him and it makes my heart happy. My daughter doesn't look much like me and I only see her a few times a year, so I don't get to really enjoy our similarities on a regular basis.

JA: What joys have you experienced? How has your life been enriched and made better having had these experiences?

AA: One of my biggest joys is having my daughter in my life. She was in my wedding, she loves my son, her half-brother, and I do get to see her mature into an amazing young lady. Her parents have been so supportive of my relationship with their entire family and they have really worked hard to keep it strong over the past fifteen years.

I also feel that my experience can help others in some way, which brings me joy. As I mentioned, this topic does not see a lot of advocacy and is rarely seen in a positive light. So, if I can help one person feel strongly about their decision and know that they may not fit in the mold society has designed for birth mothers.

JA: What advice and suggestions do you have for teens considering adoption as an option? Are there any books, movies, or other resources you feel could help them as they make a decision?

AA: I think it is one of the hardest decisions you will ever make, but it's such a positive decision. The difficulty won't disappear and it doesn't always get easier. However, it is a selfless choice. When you are pregnant, you have become a mother. A mother's job is to protect, love, and provide for her child. If you know you cannot do your job to the benefit of your child, then protect, love, and provide him or her with the opportunity to have the best life possible with a family who can.

I, personally, didn't find many resources helpful other than talking with other people who have been in my shoes. Our attempt with *Silent Embrace* is to provide birth mothers honest perspectives on placing a child—the good and the bad.

JA: Any final thoughts or words of wisdom for teens who find themselves in this situation?

AA: Trust yourself. Remember that you are no longer the priority, your baby is. Do what you can to give that baby the life he or she deserves, even if it's not with you.

Adoption is a successful, healthy, and happy reality for many people, including the children who are placed in the care of an adoptive family. Teens grappling with the decision can reflect on how much family and community support they have to raise a child, their financial situation, their education and career goals, their current and desired lifestyle, and their dreams for their child's future in order to make a decision in the best interests of themselves and their child.

making the decision to parent, it's important to realize the immense responsibilities and need for absolute accountability that parenting brings, especially to teens. Understanding exactly how tough the journey and obstacles ahead may be can help teens develop strategies to better position themselves, their child, and their families for success. Knowing what's working against teen parents is only part of the equation, though. The other part is having specific tools and resources available to combat the struggles they'll inevitably face, which is why teen parents will find suggestions, stories, and a variety of local, regional, and national resources cited throughout the rest of this book. Because, in the event teens do not have a network of supportive adults ready to help and to lean upon, they'll have to go outside their comfort zones and create a network themselves by reaching out to

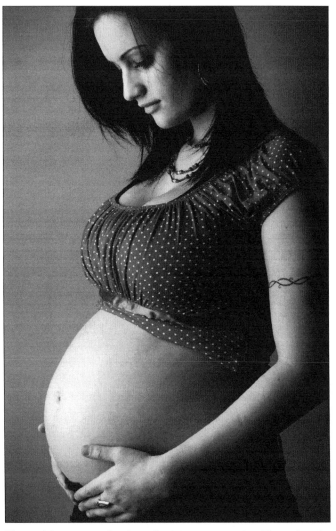

The odds are stacked against teen parents. Choosing to parent comes with a myriad of very real obstacles that teen moms and dads need to consciously address and work through in order to be successful.

local, regional, and national organizations for help. In order to work and finish their educational goals, teens may have to make sacrifices in terms of the time they can invest with their child in the short term, which will help long term, or accept help from people and institutions.

Following are only a few of the issues teens may face, but they are the most frequently cited for having the largest negative impact on teens' long-term success as individuals and within young families. Due to the weight they carry in positively or negatively impacting the lives of those choosing to parent as teens, each receives more focus and attention as this book unfolds to hopefully provide teens with the insight and inspiration they need to circumvent these challenges and rise above the negative statistics.

Lack of Involved Fathers

This is one of the biggest and most significant issues to overcome as a teen parent. Fathers financially abandon their pregnant partners 76 percent of the time and pay, on average, less than $2,000 annually in child support.[23] In a study examining

Teen Dads Only

A former teen dad known as WiseTeenDad through his blog helps teens navigate the hardships and drama of teen pregnancy through his website WiseTeenDad.com. In his article, "My Girlfriend Is Pregnant?!" WiseTeenDad speaks directly to teen dads, imploring them to be strong enough to make the tough decisions necessary to be part of, and raise, a family. From running away, to breaking up, and getting married, he addresses the fear, guilt, and regret teen fathers often feel and experience when dealing with an unexpected pregnancy. A solid read with great one-liners like, "If you decide to leave your girlfriend and new baby high and dry, I promise you will feel like a piece of trash," and "Even if you and baby mama have a hard time with each other, you need to be there for your baby and be as pleasant as you can to baby mama. The way you treat her will profoundly affect your child," and "You'll need to be a steady and strong father figure for your child," and "You don't need to have all the answers right now. Nobody really does, and nobody expects you to."[m]

father involvement with 134 children of adolescent mothers over the first ten years of life, researchers found that father-child contact was associated with better socioemotional and academic functioning. What's this mean? It means that kids with dads who showed up, were involved, and participated in the daily lives of their kids had fewer behavioral issues and did better on reading achievement tests.[24] Kids with dads who were involved in their lives were even more likely to get As![25] It's not just about the kids, either—the mothers themselves do better when they have the emotional and financial support of the father and have a better chance at finishing high school and going on to pursue more advanced educational goals.

Lack of Education

Considering putting off your education in order to take care of baby or because you can't deal with all the judgments and scrutiny as a teen parent? You might want to think again. Only 38 percent of teen mothers finish high school, and less than 2 percent of those girls earn a college degree by age thirty.[26] Dropping out of high school may set teens up for few to no employment options, as many employers and postsecondary education institutions require a high school diploma—not a GED—as a basic job qualification. Having a high school diploma shows employers and potential colleges, universities, and tech schools that teens have the basic skills needed to function within a system of rules and requirements, and that they are capable of meeting expectations (i.e., a job). In many careers, a high school diploma isn't enough. What about those teen parents who decide to pursue education past high school? They often find themselves with more opportunities, higher paying jobs, and connections and networks that advance their thinking, status, and financial well-being.

Dads: Figure Out Your Terms

According to research compiled by DoSomething.org, a site dedicated to making the world "suck less" for young people, teen fathers are stepping it up to be with their kids and they should define for themselves what "being involved" means for them and their family. "Despite the stereotypes, there is increasing evidence that teen fathers want to be (and are) involved with their children, though this involvement may not always include financial support."[n]

Economic and Financial Challenges

Onesies. Socks. Diapers. Formula. Bottles. Stroller. Diaper bag. Saving for college. Medicine. Soap and lotion. High chair. Toys. Those teeny tiny nail clippers. It all adds up, and according to BabyCenter.com, the average cost of caring for a child in his or her first year of life is $10,158.[27] That's not even including child care, a breast pump, or baby swing. Legal working age requirements and lack of education, compounded by the inability to find and obtain quality child care, can lead to situations where teens do not have the financial ability to provide for themselves, let alone their child—which is why teen childbearing in the United States cost taxpayers (federal, state, and local) at least $9.4 billion in 2010, according to an analysis by the National Campaign to Prevent Teen and Unplanned Pregnancy. Most of the costs of teen childbearing are associated with negative consequences for the children of teen mothers, including increasing costs for health care, foster care, incarceration, and lost tax revenue.[28]

Lack of Future Life Planning

Having a vision for one's life is crucial to taking the steps necessary to achieve hopes, dreams, and goals. Teens with a future life plan that includes educational, career, and family goals are better able to make decisions in their lives that guide them toward their vision. Life planning includes having an idea of how many children teens want and when they'd prefer to have a child after their unplanned pregnancy. Knowing this allows teens to choose the birth control and contraceptive method that best supports their future vision. Having no plan can result in repeated unplanned pregnancies. Many teens have the perception and mind-set that once they have the baby, they aren't going to have sex again. However, it may be unwise to think that once you've had sex, you won't ever have it again. About 25 percent of teen moms have a second child within two years of the first birth.[29] That's why a plan and strategy become so important. Teens in the United States and Europe have similar levels of sexual activity. However, European teens are more likely than U.S. teens to use contraceptives generally and to use the most effective methods; they therefore have substantially lower pregnancy rates.[30] Choosing to get pregnant at a time and interval that best fits a teen's life and long-term goals can provide teens with hope for their futures and motivation to succeed.

Having a child and raising a child are two of the most rewarding and most difficult endeavors a person can embark upon in his or her lifetime. Unfortunately, an unplanned pregnancy can make any person's journey more difficult and even unmanageable. Teens, however, may find it exceptionally challenging because they don't always have the financial, personal, or social resources to care for the child.

Teens may find themselves in the position of asking themselves if they are ready to be a parent and to take on the responsibility of raising a child. If they are, another question they may be considering is if they have the right support system in place to help them navigate starting a family. It's a time of deep personal reflection, incredible inner honesty, and often, a time of loss, pain, and grief. Teens must ultimately make a decision, and accept the full weight of that decision, that best reflects their goals for their lives and the lives of their children.

FACING JUDGMENTS, CRITICISM, AND SOCIAL STIGMAS

Among the hardest challenges of a teen pregnancy are the social issues that surround a pregnant teen and the father. In her article "Judgement of Teen Moms" for *Teen Ink*, Abby K. encourages bystanders to be kind to teen moms: "Often times the teens are embarrassed to walk outside with big stomachs, so they stay home and avoid social contact as much as possible. Unfortunately, this sometimes means they do not go for checkups with the doctors and do not take prenatal vitamins to help their babies, putting the unborn child and the mother at risk for serious health complications."[1] A teenager may also suffer an emotional crisis when she becomes pregnant, due to worry about societal disdain, which may cause her to not want the baby. This crisis may lead to rash behavior such as attempting to self-abort the baby or a suicide attempt.

When talking about social issues, this book isn't referring to the litany of social problems teen pregnancy is deeply associated with: poverty, child abuse, father absence, low birth weight, high dropout rates, and poor workplace preparation.[2] Although these problems are incredibly important to be aware of as a teen parent in order to address and potentially overcome the consequences of an unplanned pregnancy, this book is referring to the following social problems teens often face: anxiety, self-consciousness, impulsivity, and insecurity. These problems are considered age-appropriate issues most, if not all, teens face given their brain maturation process. However, pregnant teens and teen parents, wrought with these same anxieties and insecurities, must deal with an added layer of judgments, criticisms, and condemnation from their immediate family members, friends, and the greater community brought on by their decision to parent.

This chapter will share strategies on how to handle conflict and criticism, manage an emotional crisis, and understand how to look within for strength and determination.

Teens may find it hard to make prenatal doctor appointments, attend classes, or maintain their friendships for fear they will be openly or covertly judged.

Dealing with the Critics

As Babauta indicates (see below), people criticize and give unwanted opinions and advice for an endless list of reasons. Teen parents can find themselves entrenched in feedback, and wading through it all and defending themselves could become their full-time gig. Fortunately, they don't have to. They can pick and choose

---

! Inspiration for the Road Ahead

• Author, writer, and popular inspirational blogger Leo Babauta writes that people need to have hope and confidence in their journeys because it's inevitable that others will not always be as supportive as we'd hope for them to be. "You'll be criticized, because you'll make mistakes, because some will be jealous, because people have opinions about anything interesting, because people want to help you, because some want to drag down those doing anything different."[a]

the nuggets of gold they may unearth, but teens have to first take a good look at themselves and develop an arsenal of tactics in order to not get defensive and to discern the good feedback from the bad.

Understand Differences between Criticism and Helpful Advice

There are two primary types of criticism, constructive and destructive. Constructive criticism may often come across as negative, but when the recipients of the feedback take a step back, they are able to see that the feedback is helpful and, if accepted, could make a positive change in their lives. Destructive criticism, on the other hand, is meant to discourage, hurt, and bring the recipient down. Being able to differentiate and figure out if someone is trying to be helpful or hurtful can be key. For example, a teacher, employer, or parent typically wants you to be your best self, whether it's academic, on the job, or personal. The feedback on the surface may seem harsh, but could come from a place of trying to help. Friends, acquaintances, and sometimes even family members can displace their anger, resentment, or insecurities about the situation and use the guise of "giving advice" as a way to take a stab at teen parents. By focusing on what people are saying, instead of how they are saying it or even why they are saying what they are saying, you can better position yourself to respond and either internalize and use the feedback, or politely say, "Thank you for the advice" in the most genuine and authentic way you can.

Teen Mom Deals with Guilt

Chelsea H. got pregnant at seventeen and had her baby at eighteen. She struggles greatly with the guilt of not being able to provide the kind of life she had for her child: "I was watching home videos recently and I'm sad I can't give my daughter what I had," she writes. She also struggles with the shame she feels from being a teen mom. "I'm not proud of being a teen mom at all. I feel ashamed when I tell people how old I am. . . . When they hear I'm eighteen and have a baby they just do that 'oh.' . . . It really sucks." Her feelings cause her to consider adoption because she isn't sure she's "fit to be a mom."[b]

Look for Your Part in the Problem or Issue

Taking stock of what part you play in the situation, besides "victim," will help on several levels. First, acknowledge the choices made that led to becoming a teen parent. Does that mean you should be judged and criticized? No. But it does mean you have unfortunately opened yourself up to a little more feedback than the average teen. So, you should, as rapper Ice Cube says, "Check yo self before you wreck yo self."[3] Instead of reacting in a defensive manner and telling off the person offering advice, you could take a deep breath and acknowledge you're where you are because, for better or worse, you chose to be there. Not playing the victim gives you ownership for the pregnancy and for your decision to parent. Taking ownership of feelings, thoughts, and actions provides you with incredible benefits: greater pride and self-confidence, better work ethic, increased creativity, stronger learning aptitude, and, overall, a deeper awareness of yourself. If you accept your decision to parent and take responsibility for where you are, you will intrinsically feel better about yourself and your situation. Sometimes, just that level of confidence and acceptance can ward off external commentary!

Once you take ownership and admit you have a role in the problem or issue, you can take a moment to ignore the tone and ask yourself, is there any truth to what the naysayer is saying? For example, if your parents are on your case for not pulling your weight around the house, you could honestly ask yourself if you are doing everything you can to help out instead of assuming your parents are out to get you.

Play a Bigger Role in Solving the Problem

Let's say your biology teacher gives you a C on your lab report. Your initial reaction was a defensive one: that she hates you, thinks you're stupid, and thinks you can't write. After taking some time to reflect, you realize she was giving constructive feedback and maybe there was some truth to her feedback of "Grade could be improved by using more comparative scientific findings." Now, what do you do? The grade was already logged, and you're convinced the teacher doesn't want you to argue.

Maybe you're right, but sometimes, righting a wrong (in this case a C on your biology report) takes stepping up and doing whatever you can to solve the problem—in this example, acknowledging to the person you wronged (biology teacher) that he or she was right (you could do more research) and you'd like to address his or her feedback (in other words, you'd like to change). You may not be able to rewrite the paper, but you could make sure you do more research in

Self-Reflection

Getting feedback, especially unsolicited, is never fun. It can cause a lot of yucky feelings to rise to the surface: insecurity, anxiety, and fear. Feedback feels even worse when we're blind-sided because we didn't even realize our weaknesses or areas of improvement! Awareness can be key to responding to criticism. For example, if the criticism is surrounding something you care about changing, you can actively listen and see if there's some value in the feedback. If the criticism is not applicable to an area of your life you're currently trying to change, then you can still hear the person out, but with less emotional involvement.

- What are the top five areas of your life where you'd like to improve? Another way to think about this is asking yourself what your top five weaknesses or imperfections are.
- Prioritize the list in order from most important to change to least.
- Focusing on just your top three, make a list of the things you could do each day, for each weakness, that would make a positive difference. For example, if one of your weaknesses is bad grades, something that you could do daily would be to study. Messy room? You could take five minutes per day to straighten your room. Not helping around the house? Ask what you can do to be more helpful and then do it right away.
- Once you have your list for the top three, share it with someone close to you. Share that you're trying to make some positive changes. This will help you feel accountable and even more likely to achieve success.
- When you feel like you've mastered your top three, move on to the last two on your list. Keep repeating this process, and you'll be amazed at how quickly you can make self-improvements.

the future and maybe even have the teacher look over your next report and offer feedback before you submit.

When teens realize criticism is constructive, they can make a positive difference in their lives by taking an active role in honoring the feedback by making changes in their routines, behaviors, and actions.

Your Feedback Helps!

Knowing the areas of our lives where we're a little less than perfect can help us say, "Yeah, I know I'm not so great at [enter area of improvement], but I'm working on it. Your feedback helps!" Saying, "Your feedback helps!"—whether it's true or not in the moment—is great for a few reasons. One, it allows the other person to feel heard. When people feel heard, they are less likely to hit the "repeat" button and keep hounding you with their advice. Two, it allows you to positively end the conversation and allow yourself the opportunity to reflect on what they said. Maybe in the moment you're thinking, "This person is annoying or crazy," but later, you could come to realize there was some truth in his or her words. Ending the conversation on a positive note allows you to go back and thank him or her for the advice and helps deepen and build relationships.

Focus on a Strong Offense

Getting criticized can make people feel less than, vulnerable, and exposed. When people feel threatened, put down, or marginalized, they tend to get defensive. Being defensive isn't helpful in a conversation, especially in a critical conversation, because it tends to increase tension, anger, and frustrations.

Try on a more positive criticism hat for size. Instead of seeing criticism as negative and a sign of failure, try and see criticism as someone expressing feedback that can make life richer. Feedback provides an opportunity to learn and grow. Criticism can make the recipient aware of weaknesses that could be clouding hidden strengths, undiscovered talents, and more exciting life options. If the first reaction to feedback is to take it personally, aggressively disagree, prove the other person wrong, or point out why the other person is actually not so great himself or herself, then there won't be an opportunity to learn or grow. Take some time to understand how you're feeling about the feedback. Are you angry or sad? Ask yourself why. Taking the time to get yourself emotionally prepared will better enable you to hear the other person out and even learn more about yourself and how you can grow. You can even share with the naysayer how the feedback is making you feel. Being open with your emotions can help other people better

---

Teen Mom Struggles to Sympathize

Even mothers who were teen mothers themselves can struggle when their teen daughters become pregnant because, having been through the trials of teen pregnancy, they understand too well the difficult challenges their daughters are about to face. Kate Walker was seventeen when she got pregnant and eighteen when she had her daughter. Fast forward eighteen years when her eighteen-year-old daughter became pregnant. "She knew better. Yes, I had been a teenage mother, but I never expected that this would be the fate of my daughter as she saw at first hand the penalty I paid," Kate says. She also found herself unable to console her daughter. "I was ashamed of my inability to feel a connection with her. I was ashamed of my inability—and lack of desire—to comfort her. I was ashamed that my daughter was pregnant. I was ashamed of how ashamed I felt."[c]

---

understand who you are and can even make him or her more compassionate when sharing feedback in the future with others.

Set Some Boundaries

Boundaries are limits you set for yourself and for how others interact and treat you. As Jane Collingwood wrote in her article "The Importance of Personal Boundaries," boundaries "set the limits for acceptable behavior from those around you, determining whether they feel able to put you down, make fun, or take advantage of your good nature."[4] Having boundaries doesn't mean you're a jerk. It actually is a sign of personal maturity and provides a significant amount of self-esteem. People who set boundaries have a clear understanding of themselves and what they need out of life and from others to be successful and happy. This doesn't mean they are self-indulged either—having a great awareness of one's own boundaries helps a person understand and respect others' boundaries as well. For example, you might not know this about yourself, but you probably feel like there is a right time and place for feedback, right? It's probably not in the middle of a pep rally or book discussion in English class. If someone decides to share his or her thoughts on how you could have avoided your current situation and offers advice for your future, and it's at a time that isn't good for you because it's in a public setting and makes you feel embarrassed, you can set a boundary. Politely, calmly, and with respect, you can thank the person for being willing to share his or her advice, but that you'd like to talk about it at a different time. Other great responses are, "I see you have some concerns (or misunderstandings). I'd like to talk with you about that during the break," or "We all have our own opinions—we'll just have to agree to disagree this time around."

Sometimes you won't know a boundary has been hit until someone smashes into it. In those instances, it's important to think of how you feel. If it's important for you not to feel that way again, talk to the person and try to come up with solutions. Does a friend always want to give her advice on how to parent? Share with her that you're not in a place where that's all you want to talk about and suggest some different conversation topics.

Emotional Crisis Management

Life is wrought with situations, challenges, and confrontations that can create personal and emotional crises for people. Death of a loved one, job loss, debilitating car accidents, terminal illnesses, unplanned pregnancies, and even situations that are seemingly inconsequential to some such as failing a class, getting kicked off a team, and ending a long-term relationship can be emotionally overwhelming and have a dramatic impact on a person's ability to cope. Signs of emotional crisis are as diverse as individuals, but many in the throes of crisis may experience depression, anxiety, the inability to think straight, lack of self-confidence and motivation, impatience, and irritability. Signs can be more external as well, such as lack of or increased appetite, changes in sleeping patterns, suicidal thoughts, and headaches or stomach pains.[5]

These feelings can be all consuming and so overwhelming they elicit feelings of helplessness; however, if you are experiencing any of these symptoms, it's crucial you reach out to a qualified professional, doctor, loved one, or close friend for support and to start to break the cycle of unhappiness and discontent.

Fear, denial, and guilt are common emotions that surface when teens find out and then cope with their pregnancies. Understanding some of the primary emotions that can spur an emotional crisis can help teens to regain control of and manage their emotions in order to make the best decisions possible for their lives and the lives of their children.

Fear

Do any of the following worries sound familiar?

What If Someone Is Just Being a Good Ol' Fashioned Jerk?

Up to this point, the focus has been primarily on accepting criticism because it's probably well founded and useful. But this will unfortunately not always be the case. There will be times where people are simply mean, irrational, and cruel, using "feedback" as a way to hurt and cut you down. A quick way out of the conversation is to thank the person for his or her feedback, ask for an opportunity to think about it, and provide a time frame for when you'll get back to him or her. If that doesn't deter the deter-er though, the following phrases could be helpful in getting out of the conversation quickly and with your pride still intact:

- Phew. This conversation is getting heated. Maybe we can cool off a bit and then talk about it later?
- This conversation is making me feel [enter the feeling], and I don't think I can really talk about it now. Can we talk about something else for a while?
- That's a really great point you made. I don't have a good answer right now. Can I think about it and get back to you?

You can see clearly that all these phrases have something in common—they seek to end the conversation. Be clear that you're looking to move on from the topic. This will help the other person know that you're not in the right place to discuss. If he or she keeps pressing you, you can simply say, "This is not a good time for me. I feel like you're pressuring me to talk about something I'm not ready to talk about. Is this the case?" If he or she keeps up, you may have to remove yourself from the situation or setting completely. As hard as it may be, remember to always try to remain calm and collected.

- "My parents are going to kill me!"
- "I'm going to get kicked out of school!"
- "My dad is going to murder my boyfriend!"
- "I'll never amount to anything."
- "This is going to ruin my life."

- "I have to have an abortion before anyone finds out."
- "I'm not ready to be a parent. I can't do this."

People fear what they don't know, and an unplanned pregnancy brings up many unknowns—teens don't fully know themselves or their parenting abilities, they don't know how people are going to react upon finding out about the pregnancy, and they don't know what their future holds. All they know is the deep and consuming feeling of fear, which can be paralyzing and prevent them from taking positive steps. In its article "The Pregnant Teen's Dilemma," Focus on the Family reminds teens and their parents that fear and anxiety often spring from the feelings of loss everyone involved is experiencing: "The adolescent with a crisis pregnancy probably sees nothing but loss on the horizon—loss of love, time, education, and physical health. Fear of one or more of these losses propels most of her other responses."[6]

Fear can lead teens to make unhealthy choices like self-harm through suicide or self-terminating the pregnancy. It is absolutely critical that if teens feel this way that they reach out to someone, anyone, to share their fears. Talking about fears takes the power away from them. This may seem like it makes no sense; why should someone share deep, dark fears and horrible feelings with another person? Teens may worry that sharing will make their fears and worries even more potent. This line of thinking is actually fear itself holding the person back. A study done by University of Chicago psychology professor Sian Beilock, PhD, and graduate student Gerardo Ramirez, found the opposite was the case! In their study, they found simply writing about one's worries before a high-stakes exam can boost test scores. "We showed that simply getting high school students to spend 10 minutes before a high-stress exam putting their worries down on paper led to increased test performance—boosting the grades of those students who professed to have the most test anxiety from a B− to a B+," writes Beilock in her article "The Power of Expressing Yourself."[7] Beilock maintains that talking about fears can help people get rid of them, and the more expressive and articulate people are about how their fears make them feel, the better their chances of getting rid of the fear.

Denial

Denial is a defense mechanism used as a way to protect oneself from having an emotional crisis or from having to deal with unpleasant thoughts or feelings.[8] Denial is by far one of the most common defense mechanisms and happens when a person refuses to accept reality or fact, such as a pregnant teen not admitting even to herself she is pregnant. Teens may deny the fact they are pregnant in order not to deal with the stress that results from having to acknowledge and admit they are pregnant. If they simply refuse to accept the reality of their situation, they don't have to tell their parents, make a decision about whether to keep the baby, decide what they will do about school, figure out how to parent—the list of stressful decisions to make and responsibilities to accept goes on. Pregnancy denial takes many forms: misunderstanding the pregnancy for something else, like a tumor or clot; not physically looking pregnant due to a hormone imbalance, so not fully believing it's possible; and not feeling pregnant or maternal so being unable to believe the maturing physical signs are due to pregnancy.[9] Any level of denial can lead to horrific endings for pregnant teens. There are countless news articles about teens secretly delivering their babies and then hiding the babies or abandoning them, resulting in the teen parents facing neglect, abandonment, abuse, and even murder charges.

Teens often feel like they are alone and like no one could possibly understand the emotions and crisis-like situation an unplanned and unwanted pregnancy

Pregnancy: A Social Experiment

The shame and guilt teens feel is real and often brought on by seemingly well-meaning friends and family. In an effort to "help," many offer judgments and insults instead. Oregon-based Forest Grove High School senior Maria Miranda lived in an area where many girls found themselves pregnant as teens, and she felt they were getting unfairly and unjustly treated by peers and adults. Inspired by the 2012 movie and 2013 memoir *The Pregnancy Project*, and wanting to better understand the experiences pregnant teens were facing, Maria underwent a social experiment for six months and pretended to be pregnant. Although there were a few supportive friends, the responses she received as a pregnant teen were heartbreaking. She was called stupid and irresponsible. She lost several friends and many students wouldn't even make eye contact with her. One teacher even remarked, to her face, "Oh great. A child having a child." Maria was lucky since she could end the ruse at any time, whereas teen parents can't, but she learned a great deal and gained a significant amount of compassion for pregnant teens. "We all make mistakes," Maria said. "Not only teen moms." She added, there's also the mistakes of those who judge them.[d]

can bring on. Arnetta Stewart, a teen mother of two, hid her second pregnancy because she was ashamed that she had gotten pregnant again. According to a news article by *Philly.com*, Stewart now works with pregnant teens who share the same feelings she experienced. "When you're a teen-ager, you think you're the only one going through it," she said and encouraged teens to tell their parents. "There's no relationship that's more important than that. . . . It's not going to disappear."[10]

If sharing with parents or a primary caregiver isn't an option, teens can help themselves manage the feelings of panic and dread by talking to an adviser or teacher, doctor or medical professional, member of their religious community, or another trusted adult.

Guilt

In its article "The Pregnant Teen's Dilemma," Focus on the Family writes, "When a pregnancy results from the violation of moral values held since childhood, an adolescent will usually feel ashamed and worthless. Her growing abdomen becomes a constant reminder of her failure."[11] Teens can feel a deep sense of guilt for the pregnancy, and if left unchecked, excessive feelings of guilt can lead to resentment and depression.

Certain levels of guilt aren't all that bad. Guilt reminds us that we've made a poor choice and that we are remorseful for our actions. Being remorseful and sorry for our actions allows us to assess where we went wrong and how we can make sure we don't make the same actions or repeat the same behaviors in the

---

Look Within for Positivity

John Preston, licensed psychologist and author of twenty-one books, offers four key tactics to see the positive in guilt and not let guilt turn glum:

1. Ask yourself the following questions:
   a. What do I think of myself?
   b. What am I telling myself?
   c. How do I feel as though I am to blame?
   d. What do I feel shame about?

2. Identify everything about the situation that you are primarily responsible for in bullet points and why you are specifically feeling guilty about it.

3. For each bullet point, ask yourself if what you wrote is true. Are you really completely responsible or were there perhaps some other contributing factors you need to consider?

4. Once you have a better idea of your role and maybe what you need to take responsibility for, or what you're overly beating yourself up about, he suggests thinking about the following:

   a. Own up and, if needed, apologize or make other amends, as appropriate.

   b. Think about your intentions. Did you mean to cause pain, trouble, or issues? Probably not, so make sure you understand what your intent was and take solace in the fact that while you may be in the situation you're in because of choices you made, your intentions were never to hurt anyone.

   c. Transform guilt to regret. Guilt sucks because it makes us feel like bad people. Regret allows us to see our mistakes as just mistakes and areas for improvement instead of failures.

   d. Make a list of all the great things about yourself. What are your strengths? Positive characteristics? Are you smart and giving? Do you help others? Reflect on all the good you've done and focus on making positive changes in your life instead of fixating on the negative choices you may or may not have made.[e]

future. The repentant side of guilt can help us take responsibility for our actions, which is a positive skill.

What gets us into trouble is when guilt gets dark, we begin to take more blame than deserved, and instead of making positive changes, we stop trying to understand and solve the problem at hand.

Not dwelling on feelings of guilt, denial, and fear can help pregnant teens move forward and lead healthier, more fulfilling lives. Seeing themselves as soon-to-be parents instead of big mistake makers, failures, and bad people provides strength and confidence to learn more about parenting, raising children, and being the best version of themselves.

Inner Strength

Teen parents often struggle with the pressures of raising children, and research shows it's largely due to their age and inadequate number of life experiences and coping skills. Teens who give up on their educational dreams to parent often resent their decision, and the research shows they end up being harsher parents.[12]

Age and a longer life bring some pretty incredible benefits to adults: self-knowledge of strengths and weakness, maturity, and self-confidence. Adults—through the trial, error, and learning curves of their lives and experiences—have developed the ability to confront and navigate challenges and opportunities that teens typically cannot. Teens can find themselves feeling overly judged—both from external pressures and from themselves—because they aren't quite ready to parent, but they *are* parents. But just because teens are at an experiential disadvantage doesn't mean they should give up, cave to the statistics, and stop trying to reduce the gap between where they are and could be.

Educating themselves on child development and parenting strategies, together with having a strong family plan and taking good care of themselves emotionally, physically, and spiritually can help provide teens with a sense of control and power in a situation that all too often makes them feel powerless and small.

Child Development

The first few years of a child's life are crucial to his or her emotional, psychological, and physical well-being and success. A loving and supportive home environment and proper hygiene, medical care, and nutrition are key elements in ensuring positive child development. Teens raising a child or family can benefit

Child Development Milestones

The Centers for Disease Control and Prevention offers extensive resources, materials, and multimedia tools such as videos on what milestones are typical for children from two months of age until five years. There's even a printable checklist for parents to track and better understand the important skills their child is building as they play, learn, speak, and move. Check it out at http://www.cdc.gov/ncbddd/actearly/milestones/index.html.

from researching development milestones. Understanding when key development milestones typically occur in the life of a child—like latching on or being able to take a bottle and keep food down, smiling for the first time, sitting up, rolling over, standing, taking first steps, saying those first few words, and more—will help parents be able to nurture and support these behaviors.

In the event a child is not hitting key milestones, parents that understand when they are typically supposed to occur, can monitor their child more closely and then speak with their health care provider or pediatrician about their child and the missed or delayed milestone. This level of involvement and understanding about development milestones can not only encourage a bond between parent and child, but also prevent or catch any delays and allow parents and health care providers to develop a plan to overcome any delays if necessary.

Parenting Strategies

Parenting strategies are the conscious decisions parents make on how they want to raise their child or children. A person's parenting strategy encompasses every single decision he or she makes regarding how his or her child is brought up and raised, including

- discipline techniques;
- rule setting and enforcement;
- religious, moral, or spiritual upbringing;
- new skill development;
- educational decisions and preferences;
- and so many more elements of parenting!

Seem overwhelming? It can be. That's why there are hundreds of books, each as varied and unique as the people in the world, dedicated to virtually every element, facet, and aspect of parenting. Teens should take time while they are pregnant to research parenting and develop their own set of standards and strategies about the kind of parent they aspire to be. Things to research can include

- age appropriate expectations and behaviors;
- effective discipline;
- establishing rules and expectations around home, school, and social life;
- negative consequences for undesirable behavior;
- encouraging good behavior and reward systems;
- bedtime routines;
- potty training.

And there are many, many more. It's easy to get overwhelmed by the sheer number of things to think about and plan for as a parent, but remember that's why there are experts out there you can reach out to. Medical professionals, child psychologists, friends with kids the same age as your child, your parents or caregivers, and even educators can help you define and enforce a parenting strategy you can be proud of.

Family Management Plan

A family management plan includes knowing the number of children you'd like to conceive, when you'd like your next child, and the spacing (or how far apart they are) between each. While teens experiencing unplanned pregnancies may initially feel like they don't want another baby and will never have sex again, this may be an unreasonable long-term strategy once baby comes and teens heal from the birth.

Teens may truly never feel like they are ready and may not know right away if they want another child, let alone the spacing between each, so another part of the family management plan is being able to prevent a repeat unwanted pregnancy.

Teens without a family management plan or an understanding of how far apart they'd like their children are at an increased risk for a repeat unplanned pregnancy, putting them even further away from their educational or career goals. Don't think this applies to you? Think again: almost 25 percent of teens will have a second child within two years of their first.[13]

Pregnancy Prevention Options

Every person—whether you're female or male—is different. That's why there are so many diverse contraceptives and protection methods out there. Some birth control methods can only be obtained through a prescription from a medical professional, while others are available at local drugstores or pharmacies.

A report completed by the National Campaign to Prevent Teen and Unplanned Pregnancy stated that in the United States, women using no contra-

---

❗ Morally Acceptable? Only You Can Determine

● A May 2012 Gallup poll found that 89 percent of adults, including 87 percent of Republicans, 90 percent of Democrats, and 82 percent of Catholics found the use of birth control morally acceptable.[f]

> ## Contraceptive Use Rates
>
> ● Ninety-nine percent of American women who have ever had sex have used contraception at some point in their lives, as have 98 percent of Catholic women.[9]

ception or using it inconsistently account for 52 and 43 percent of unplanned pregnancies, respectively.[14] Similar proportions are found for abortions. You're wondering about the importance of this, well, here it is: only 5 percent of unplanned pregnancies result from method failure.[15] Five percent. This proportion of unplanned pregnancies and abortions based on women using no contraception is particularly striking given that they account for only 8 percent of women at risk of an unplanned pregnancy.[16]

From birth control patches, pills, shots, sponges, and rings, to condoms, diaphragms, IUDs, and morning-after pills, the sheer number of contraceptives available can be overwhelming. And that is just getting an idea for what's out there, not getting into how each works or the success rate of one method over another.

There are many factors in determining what level and type of protection is the best fit, from wanting protection from sexually transmitted infections or pregnancy and needing protection from both sexually transmitted infections and unintended pregnancy, to not being able/willing to take a pill daily, being allergic to latex, and not being able/willing to see a health care professional for a prescription.

Not sure where to start? Check out My Method, provided by Planned Parenthood. For almost one hundred years, Planned Parenthood has been an advocate for millions of women and men through its efforts to provide reproductive health care and sex education. Not to be used as a replacement for a discussion with a medical professional, but as a way to research and gain knowledge, My Method

Head Online

Find My Method at www.plannedparenthood.org/all-access/my-method-26542.htm. For more information on the various methods and their effectiveness, call Planned Parenthood at 1-800-230-PLAN.

presents a series of questions and then suggests potential birth control options based on your answers.

A family plan and an awareness and commitment to preventing another unwanted pregnancy are key components to teens being able to beat the statistics and pursue their hopes, dreams, and goals. Another way teens can help themselves prosper and grow, thus helping their child and family, is to practice strong self-care.

Self-Care

Parenting is a full-time job, and there are no comprehensive user manuals on how to be the perfect parent. That's why so many books are dedicated to the subject, and these books vary wildly in terms of content. Parenting involves making many mistakes, constantly learning, having unlimited patience and understanding, and also having the energy and wherewithal to keep up with an itty bitty! Parenting is hard work and requires parents to step back from the day-to-day grind and practice some self-care.

Self-care is how we nurture and develop our own personal health and well-being. Although it's incredibly hard to practice self-care with an infant given the lack of sleep, demands of taking care of and feeding baby, and any feelings of anxiety or sadness over the new normal life is taking with baby, it's crucial in these moments for new moms to take a little time to also care for themselves. Pregnancy is a good time to set habits around self-care so that once the baby comes, you'll be more likely to maintain the time set aside for you to recharge and reduce stress levels. The following are areas where greater self-care may be needed during pregnancy and once baby arrives:

Getting Some Exercise

Consistent exercise does wonders for the body: improves circulation, boosts the immune system, and makes you feel good. Exercise doesn't have to be strenuous, cost a ton of money, or require fancy equipment either. A walk a few times around the block with baby in the stroller, jogging up and down the stairs while baby sleeps, or even doing pull-ups on the monkey bars at a local playground while kids play can constitute a solid workout. Search "at home workouts" on the Internet, and millions of programs pop up for building muscle, increasing fitness, and losing weight. Libraries also house many books, videos, and magazines on exercise for free.

Eating Healthy

This can be difficult, especially for teens on a budget or those living at home and not in charge of the grocery shopping. However, proper nutrition is key for a developing pregnancy and postbirth. Good nutrition is key for those teens who choose to breastfeed. Taking the recommended prenatal pills during pregnancy and a multivitamin postbirth can provide nutrients and minerals often lacking from most diets.

Resting

An ever-expanding waistline, surges of hormones, and frequent trips to the bathroom can lead to pregnant moms yearning for a full night's rest. While one

Healthy Eating Resources

Not sure what healthy eating constitutes? Check out the following online resources to educate yourself:

- Berkeley Wellness. This site offers countless resources, including "14 Keys to a Healthy Diet." www.berkeleywellness.com/
- Mayo Clinic. Full of health and wellness resources, the Mayo Clinic's website has a treasure trove of information on dietary guidelines, nutritional overviews, and definitions on terms. www.mayoclinic.org/
- U.S. Department of Agriculture. From recipes, cookbooks, menus, and tips for eating out; to starting points for how to eat healthy, count calories, and increase physical activity, the USDA offers many materials to educate and inform on its ChooseMyPlate.gov website.
- Eat This, Not That! A series of books and an online community that offers seemingly endless food swaps to save calories and increase wellness. The site features articles that cover the gamut of nutrition: one-day detoxes, best foods for weight loss, foods that make you feel fuller, top nutritional tips, and more. http://www.eatthis.com/

❗ Try This! Invest in Comfy Clothes

● From BabyCenter.com: "If your breasts are sore, get a good supportive cotton bra. Maternity bras can offer extra support, so try a couple on to see whether you like them. Your breasts might increase one or two more sizes, especially if this is your first pregnancy, and a knowledgeable sales associate can help you with sizing."[h]

---

method may work for one mom-to-be or new parent and not the next, some techniques to sleep more soundly include stretching, yoga, deep breathing, a warm bath, a cup of warm milk or noncaffeinated tea, or even investing in a body pillow or more pillows for better sleeping support. The sleeplessness may not end with the birth either. Most new parents struggle with a lack of sleep as both they and baby adjust to, well, life with baby! A good rule of thumb is to sleep when the baby sleeps, take naps, and go to bed earlier if at all possible. If you're really struggling, talk to your health care provider and discuss the potential for prescription or over-the-counter solutions.

Another area of self-care is developing and strengthening healthy relationships. This is an area teens in particular may struggle with the most due to family structures being strained over the pregnancy news, friendships ending or weakening after the baby arrives, and any relationship issues between teen mother and father.

EXPERIENCING LOST FRIENDSHIPS, RELATIONSHIPS, AND TRUST

Many teens notice a sharp decline in the number and quality of their friendships pre- and postbaby. Many teen moms also go into the pregnancy with hopes of fathers being instrumental in not only the baby's life but their own as well. Unfortunately, the statistics are not in their favor as eight out of ten fathers don't marry the mother of their child.[1] Teen fathers may go in with the best intentions, too, but struggle understanding what it means, or how, to provide for moms and their new babies. Layered onto the loss of their friends and relationships, teen parents face scrutiny and massive distrust from their parents. This fact alone could impact a father's relationship with the mother and baby as the mother's parents could prohibit the father from having any interaction.

How does a person build trust once it's lost? What can teens do to move past lost friendships and build new ones? How can teens effectively co-parent with their partner? While there are countless strategies, methods, and techniques, a

"Some people I met thought having a kid was cool, while others were uncomfortable around me. I found it hard to make friends because no one related to what I was going through or understood what it was like to have a kid. The hardest thing I had to adjust to were the looks I got when I was out with London in public. I can still see the judgment on people's faces when they realize she's my daughter and not my little sister."—Daizchane Baker, in her article "An Intimate Look at Life as a Teen Mom"[a] few are shared in this chapter to get teen parents thinking about how to build and maintain deeper relationships with the people instrumental in their lives.

Trust Can Be Tricky

In the story of the three little pigs, the wolf successfully blew down two of the three houses due to poor construction—one was built of straw and the other of sticks. The pigs who didn't have well-built houses, well, they didn't fare too well and met a gruesome fate. The house that withstood the wolf's advances and protected the final piggy was solidly built of bricks. Trust is similar to these houses. When we're honest, make decisions that are right and just, and live our lives with a sense of transparency and openness, then we build a foundation in which people can believe what we say, depend upon our actions, and be certain that we can be trusted. Our house is strong, can withstand trials and tribulations, and will be welcoming to those we love and care for. If we steal, lie, don't honor our word, and cheat others in one way or another, then our house is going to be flimsy and people we love and trust won't want to come in.

Unfortunately, it's often the case that when teens engage in sexual activity, they aren't always forthright on an astonishing variety of levels. Teens may ignore their parent or caregiver's questions and attempts to get a conversation going around their intended or actual sexual activity. Teens may lie outright and say they aren't having sex, when they actually are or plan to. Some teens may have birth control options, but fail to take them—even though they promised their parents or partner they would practice safe sex. Some teens may lie to their health care providers about their sexual activity and fail to get access to contraceptives.

❗ Try This! Develop a Mom Network

● Consider reaching out to other people, to friends and family who've had children—or are at the same stage in pregnancy as you. Making the initial connection may be scary, but according to BabyCenter.com, a lot can be gained from seeking out those who've traveled the path before you. "Women who've already made the transition to motherhood can offer good advice, a comforting shoulder, and the camaraderie of shared experiences. If you and your mother have a good relationship, she may be the best source of support. If you don't know where to start the conversation, ask your mom or a friend to tell you about her best and worst pregnancy memories."[b]

Still other teens may lie to themselves. These teens may know they intend to have sex, but ignore or pretend the potential of unintended pregnancy doesn't and couldn't apply to them. They may believe, to their detriment, getting pregnant would never happen to them.

This dishonesty isn't helpful to teens—especially teens who end up getting pregnant and then need to tell their parents. The lies they told about their sexual activity and where they were and how they got pregnant can begin to compound. This leaves teens in a desperate situation where they need a network more than ever, but due to lies, evasions, and dishonesty, they may have broken their network or be too afraid to tap into it.

When teens finally do tell their parents or caregivers, the sum of their lies catches up. They have to deal with not only the emotional rollercoaster that comes with pregnancy and being a teen, but also the result of their lies: the people they love and need the most don't trust them, disbelieve their every word, and don't see them as ever being trustworthy or responsible again.

Having dishonesty confronted and owning up to it can be a harrowing experience and leave teens feeling lost, empty, and without a clue as to how to fix their parents', loved ones', and friends' perception of them. Fortunately, with a little effort, there are several things teens can do to make great strides in building and then maintaining trust in their relationships.

Make and Keep Commitments

According to Stephen M. R. Covey, the single quickest way to build trust in any relationship is to make, and then keep, commitments. "It is the 'Big Kahuna' of all behaviors," Covey writes in his book *The Speed of Trust: The One Thing That Changes Everything.*[2] "Its *opposite*—to break commitments or violate promises—is, without question, the quickest way to destroy trust."[3] Keeping commitments shows people you are building trust with that they can trust you to follow through with what you said you were going to do. Start small. If you commit to showing up for coffee with a friend, show up. If you make a doctor's appointment, don't miss it. If you tell your parents you'll take the trash out, do it.

This can even be done with yourself. In fact, the very first person with whom teens should improve their ability to trust and be trusted is themselves! "Making and keeping commitments to yourself is the key to success in making and keeping commitments to others. That's what gives you the power and the confidence—the Self Trust—that enables you to build trust with others," writes Covey.[4]

Here's why: Many people make goals and plans they rarely achieve. This can lead to these people feeling frustrated and deflated by themselves. They can get depressed, down, and frustrated, which spills out into their relationships with

Rebuild a strained or broken relationship with parents and caregivers by actively building trust. Be patient, too. It may take more than a few days or even a few weeks to gain back the goodwill and trust lost.

others. Teens should ask themselves what they can do to improve their levels of trust with themselves. Here are some examples:

- Did you make a commitment to wake up at a certain time, yet hit the snooze button every morning? Stop. Commit to waking up and then get up at that time. Otherwise, continuing to promise yourself you'll do something, but then not actually end up doing it, can lead to feelings of inadequacy and self-doubt.
- Do you have a paper due in two weeks and know that you need to study, do some research, and then start working on the paper well enough in advance so that you'll be able to turn it in and be proud of the resulting

grade? Instead of avoiding the work, break the paper down into reasonable chunks. Commit to spending one day going over your class notes and another researching on the web or at the library, and then commit to writing one paragraph a day until the day before it's due. On that day, take some time to review what you've written, make any changes, and get the paper ready to be turned in. By confronting your problem head on—paper being due—and then not avoiding the deadline, you're teaching yourself to be honest about what you can and can't do in the given timeline. You are holding yourself accountable to your self-set deadlines and then showing yourself you can deliver on time and meet your standards.

- Do you often exaggerate or lie to friends and family to come off as better than you are? Do you always promise yourself that you'll stop trying to impress others and just be yourself? Make a mental note that when you start to hear yourself brag or boast, you'll immediately use that as a cue to stop talking about yourself—even midsentence—and ask the person you're talking to how his or her day is going. Or ask what he or she has going on the upcoming weekend. Ask him or her anything that takes the focus off yourself in order for you to collect your thoughts and stop the lie or one-upping in its tracks.
- What about promising your parents you'll be home by nine and then always missing curfew, getting in trouble, and feeling miserable that you keep messing up? Maybe set an alarm on your phone to go off thirty minutes to an hour before you need to be home and use that as a cue to head back home. Even if you're early and miss a little time with your friends, you'll feel better that you actually followed through with a commitment you made.

The most important thing you can do in a relationship where you've lost trust is to make a commitment and then keep it—without fail. Covey offers an easily repeatable process: "Find a value-added reason to make a commitment and keep it . . . and do it again . . . and again . . . and again."[5] It's important to not let people down in this process, so don't make a commitment you know you can't keep or you fear you don't have the time to keep. It's way better to make reasonable commitments, say take out the trash or do the dishes, than one you can't accomplish, like repainting the house or helping to pay the rent (if you don't have a job).

In order to gain trust and respect from their parents, teens need to display trustworthy behavior. According to Kathryn Hatter in her article "How Teens Build Trust with Parents," there are many ways teens can earn trust from parents, such as following home and school rules, acting respectfully, communicating openly, exhibiting sound judgment, and controlling impulses.[6] Being honest and taking ownership for past mistakes or lies; being transparent about where you're

Say What You Mean and Mean What You Say

Many people want to do it, but too few actually ever do. What's that? Follow through on what they say they're going to do. Effective immediately, make a pact with yourself to be one of the few, not the many, by trying out these suggestions from the blog *Little Things Matter:*

- Uphold your word with a good attitude. Remember that it was you who said yes in the first place.
- Take every opportunity to learn from your commitments so that you can make better decisions in the future.
- Finally, do you have any unfulfilled commitments? Do them now. You will feel better.[c]

going, with who, and when you'll be back; and keeping your word and commitments are key ways you can build a strong foundation of trust with your parents, loved ones, and even friends.

The Ups and Downs of Friendship

In Girl Scouts, there is a song all scouts are required to learn when they join—"Make New Friends." The lyrics praise making new friends and keeping the old ones even closer; that like a circle, friendship has no end; friendship starts from a feeling within; and together, friends can make the world a better place despite challenges and distance. While this is a simple song with a lovely end rhyme to help little ones memorize the lyrics, it contains kernels of truth many know implicitly: many of us depend on the support, love, and confidence of our friends. Whether we are social butterflies with a vast field of friends, or more introverted loners with a close few; the people we choose to spend our time and share our hearts with hold a special place in our lives.

Teens going through an unexpected and unintended pregnancy can find themselves on the outskirts of their social networks and ostracized by their peers. Many face losing their existing friendships and can feel an acute sense of loneliness without the people they once considered closest to them. Understanding how

> ## ! What Is Friendship?
>
> In *The Four Loves*, C. S. Lewis writes that "friendship is born at that moment when one person says to another: 'What! You too? I thought I was the only one.'"[d]

to deal with the loss of a friendship, changes in the closeness of a friendship, and making new friends are key life skills for teens.

When Friendships End

Friendships end for many, many reasons. Some people naturally grow apart as they age and their interests change. Friendships that grow from a love of soccer could fade as one friend takes an interest in art and the other stays soccer obsessed. Some friendships are toxic and prone to fighting, arguing, and competition, which can leave both parties frustrated and ready to cut ties. Friends can move away from one another, and distance and poor planning can lead to a disconnect; friends can meet other people who are more like them at a given time in their lives and decide to invest more time with like-minded individuals; and maybe the hardest for pregnant teens, some friends may not be okay with or respect the decisions the other is making and decide to move on from the relationship.

When friendships end or the depth of the relationship changes, it can cause teens to be confused, hurt, and feel rejected. While it can feel like the end of the world, many times, the end of one friendship can open a door and space for another, new friendship to develop. Eileen Kennedy-Moore, PhD, offers the following suggestions for dealing with a lost friendship:

- Don't let emotions be your guide. "The break-up of a friendship can be very painful," Kennedy-Moore writes in her article for *Psychology Today* titled "Make New Friends but Keep the Old . . . or Not."[7] Teens may need to take some time to manage their feelings of betrayal, anger, and confusion over the end of the friendship. Confiding their feelings about the situation with someone who is empathetic and understanding can help teens cool down, and another person hearing about what happened can also help teens see the reality of the situation with less emotion and help them move past the loss.
- Don't get nasty. Kennedy-Moore writes that teens who are angry "may be tempted to try to 'get back' at the former friend in some way. This could mean anything from hitting the other child to gossiping and telling

The end of one friendship can provide an opportunity for teens to forge a new and more fulfilling friendship. Perhaps they aren't looking to play video games all night anymore, but to connect with fellow teen fathers or even older parents who are expecting around the same time they are.

everyone at school what a rotten person the former friend is." While this initial reaction is normal and understandable, Kennedy-Moore attests that "nothing good will come of acting on it. It certainly won't repair the relationship, and it's likely to escalate the battle."[8] Teens who act out negatively or say hurtful things about their prior friend could even hurt their chances of making new friends since other peers may see them as spiteful and cruel, not characteristics most people want in a new friend.

- Give the relationship some time. "Not all friendship endings are permanent," Kennedy-Moore writes and shares that sometimes arguments that aren't that bad, and friendships that were pretty strong to begin with maybe just need a break and some space, not necessarily an end.[9] Teens whose friends initially distance themselves due to the pregnancy news may have done so initially because they didn't know how to deal with the news or support their friend. Some friends may have parents with strong opinions about teen pregnancy that can prevent them from hanging out or spending time with the pregnant teen. With time, these friendships can often redevelop if each party acts with kindness, consideration, and respect toward each other.

- Let it go. There are times, writes Kennedy-Moore, where we can't get a friendship to work, regardless of the time, effort, and energy put into it.[10] Some people just won't like each other, respect each other's decisions, or be there for each other when times get tough. In these cases, teens can take a step back from the friendship and begin to make new friends.
- Build a bigger network. "Because children's friendships often end, it makes sense to . . . have several friends, or, even better, several circles of friends," concludes Kennedy-Moore.[11] Having friends in many facets of life will help teens bounce back when a friendship in one area ends.

Making New Friends

Making new friends isn't easy, especially as a new parent, but it's critical to people of all ages to have strong friendships with like-minded peers. Teen parents

> "Wishing to be friends is quick work, but friendship is a slow ripening fruit."—Aristotle

may even find it more crucial because a strong network of relationships can help them be better parents and better able to secure and pursue their dreams and aspirations. Jessica Stevenson, teen advice expert for About.com, suggests the following tips for making new friends:

- Get inquisitive. There is nothing worse than getting to know someone and wanting to share about yourself, but the other person won't let you get a word in edgewise. Don't be that person! Get off to the best start by actively listening to what the other person is saying and then asking questions about his or her values, interests, and what he or she is involved in. You want your new friend to feel like you want to get to know him or her, and you also want to be sure your new friend is showing you the same respect and consideration. Red flags should go up for new friends who don't stop talking about themselves.
- Say something nice. Does your new friend have a great sense of style, a cool diaper bag, or an ability to do everything—parent, go to school,

and hold down a part-time gig—all at once? Share how impressed you are! Stevenson writes, "Noticing something you like about someone and sharing it with him or her is a great way to forge a connection and start a conversation."[12]

- Set the technology down. Nothing says, "I don't care what you have to say right now," like texting when you're talking to someone. Constantly being on your phone or device can also turn people off from wanting to get to know you, writes Stevenson. "You're less likely to notice who's interested in you if you're constantly checking your e-mail, voicemail and text messages. Being online or on the phone also sends the message to others that you're unavailable."[13]

- Get involved. Interested in learning how to bake, sew, or crochet? What about taking a baby birth and delivery or breastfeeding class? For the dads out there, ever consider a new fathers group? Is there a cause you want to get more involved with? Being aware of your interests or areas in which you need to learn a new skill can help you better understand what club or groups to join or organizations to volunteer at. Being part of a club or group, or volunteering, can help facilitate new friendships because you'll typically be surrounded by people with similar interests or in similar situations to yourself. They also offer even more benefits, writes Stevenson, "Clubs, teams, and other groups also work toward common goals, which is inspiring, teaches you how to solve problems, and helps you bond with others."[14]

- Make some money. "Getting a part-time job at a place where other teens work is another way to meet people and work toward common goals," writes Stevenson.[15]

- Be positive. Having a positive demeanor, smiling, and being open can help attract people toward you, making it easier to meet new people. Not many people want to be friends with a negative, grumpy, or seemingly closed-off person.

Importance of Co-parenting

While friendships are incredibly important to many people, one of the most critical relationships teens will need to nurture and develop will be the one they share with their partner—the father or mother of their child. As has been discussed throughout this book, teen parents face many challenges: financial, social, and educational, to name a few. But, as with any relationship that involves children, teens may struggle the most with their relationship with their partner. Especially since many teens do not end up in long-term, healthy relationships with

In His Words: Interview with Dad Mark/WiseTeenDad

Mark/WiseTeenDad found out his girlfriend, now wife, was pregnant at sixteen and they had their first child at seventeen. In this section he shares his story, the unique challenges teen dads face, and how to overcome some of the hardest stereotypes.

Mark/WiseTeenDad's Initial Thoughts and Reactions

Wow . . . I was dumbfounded. It was like an out of body experience. I was so scared and nervous. Initially I thought my life was over. But after a while, I actually started getting a little excited and hopeful. I thought this may be my big chance to break free from my troubled teenage life and have a real reason to be a better person than I was. I wish I would have had a better relationship with God back then, but I never really felt I had a strong purpose for living.[e]

How Mark and His Partner Broke the News

It took a while for us to process everything and discuss all of our options. At this point, I was hoping that we could make it work between us, keep our baby, and get married. She ended up telling her parents fairly quickly. Shortly after that, she ended up moving away to Oregon where her parents were going to start a new business. I obviously had to stay in Utah with my family. For the next few months, it was a whole lot of long hours spent on long distance phone calls with her discussing how we could make things work and keep our baby, or if giving him up for adoption was the better choice.

Unfortunately, I still hadn't told my parents that she was pregnant. This was a terrible decision and would have made things a lot easier for me if I'd have just bit the bullet. I had no adults in my life that I was discussing any of this with in Utah, just my teenage friends. I feel terrible about how long it took for my parents to find out. I didn't even really come out and tell them; it was about eight months into the pregnancy that a letter showed up at my house from the adoption agency that we were most likely going to use. I finally came clean with them and told them how far along she was.

How Family and Friends Reacted

Both of our parents were very hurt and disappointed. Her parents thought it was a much better idea to give our baby up for adoption to a more mature, stable family. Since mine didn't find out until the 11th hour, their reaction was even more shocked and confused. I felt so alone nearly the entire time. I experienced a lot of depression, and even had to get on medication to help for a while. Managing your feelings as a teenager, expecting a baby, is one of the most difficult things you can do. I didn't manage mine very well. I was all over the place on the emotional roller coaster! I now wish I would have had some stronger relationships with at least one or two trusted adults that I could have confided in, and more importantly, with God.

Unique Challenges for Young Fathers

Many young fathers feel like everyone else is looking down at them seeing an irresponsible piece of trash who will end up running away from their responsibilities. Whether this is perception or reality, it doesn't matter. What young fathers must come to believe is that they *are* capable of making the best of a very tough adult situation. Show everyone around you that you are going to make your baby a priority and they'll eventually respect you and whatever decisions you have made with baby momma. If you will surround yourselves with some positive adult figures to support, love, and give wise advice, things will turn out better than expected!

How Teens Can Become Strong Fathers

Use the abundant resources that are at your fingertips, like this very book! But don't just read one book . . . read five or even ten, and then do something with the knowledge you gain! Parenting websites for dads are plentiful too. Taking good advice to heart and implementing positive changes in your life to become the strongest man you can, will naturally make you a stronger father. Depending on your relationship with your own father; make an honest list of all the good (or bad) things you learned from him, and try to teach those (or the opposite) to your child. Strive to be an even better example of strength and unconditional love than your father was to you. Your child is always watching and absorbing your reactions, moods, language, and how you treat others through life's challenges. As a father, the most important gift you can give to your child is their knowledge of your unconditional love and support.

How Teen Fathers Can Build Better Relationships with Their Partners

This is tough, and takes a whole lot of patience. Probably more patience than any teenager's had to use before. You must prove to them that you will not abandon their daughter to deal with this baby alone. Show them that you really want to help make the best and most mature decision for everyone involved. Whether that is getting married and keeping the baby, or finding a loving family waiting for the chance to be parents through the incredible gift of adoption. I do not believe that abortion is an acceptable solution and would strongly encourage you to take that off your list of options immediately. The guilt and shame of that decision would haunt you for the rest of your life, I promise.

Thoughts on Finishing School and Education

I really wish I would have made education a higher priority. Yes, things have ended up working out for us financially; but I know if I had gone to more schooling it would have been a much quicker and easier road. If I could have a do over, I would definitely finish high school and immediately start in on my college classes. Even if it were just one or two classes at a time, I know that would have produced great results for me and my family.

Coping with Blame, Stigmas, and Pressure

Do not succumb to peer pressure and be careful in listening to your teenage friends' advice. As mentioned, try and surround yourself with at least one or two trusted adults and share all your feelings with them. Gaining a new perspective on life is key. Beginning to understand who we truly are and why we are here on earth will be paramount. We are all beloved children of God who wants to see us overcome all of our tests and trials, and will help us achieve that if we will just reach out and ask him through prayer. Even in the worst situations, God can help us make them bearable and eventually turn them into something positive.

How Teen Fathers Can Co-parent

If you are planning to stay together; getting a good job and working your butt off will be huge. Put away the video games for a while and prove yourself. Man up; you're stronger and more capable than you know. You need to show your girlfriend and her parents that you are committed to providing for her and your new child. Reading books and taking classes on marriage and parenting would be amazing too.

If you are not going to stay together, you still need to provide as much financial and emotional support as you can. Keeping good, healthy communication with your baby momma is so important. Offering to help as much as possible will keep you on good terms with momma and baby as they grow up. Make sure that you are never degrading to your baby's momma; that will have terrible consequences.

Mark/WiseTeenDad's Advice to Teen Fathers

You aren't alone! There are so many past and present teen fathers who have been or are going through the same thing right this instant. Draw strength from us, reach out to us, we can be a helpful resource to you! Do not suffer alone in silence, take a leap of faith and share your feelings and struggles with somebody else. You'll instantly feel a little better, just try it!

If you don't have a relationship with God, nothing can be more helpful right now. If you just say a small and simple prayer, God will let you know He is there for you. If you haven't prayed yet today (or for a long time, or ever!) try finding a quiet place, folding your arms and closing your eyes (helps block out distractions) and just begin to talk to Him. He's not just the Creator of this big crazy universe; He's also a loving and caring Father! Think about how much you love your new baby, now multiply that by infinity, and that's how much God loves you personally.

Stay strong, know that things will get better if you stay positive and tell yourself over and over that you will get through this. You will never be the same again, and whether that's a good thing or a bad thing is completely up to you. Man up and smile, your life is not over, it's just beginning an amazing new chapter! Much love, I'm praying for you and so are countless others.

You can check out Mark/WiseTeenDad's blog, www.wiseteendad.com, for more advice, his story, and resources just for teen fathers.

the mother or father of their child. Only about one out of every ten teens aged fifteen to nineteen who give birth get married.[16] Of those teen mothers who were not married when their child was born, only about 34 percent went on to marry by the time their child reached age five.[17] This means most teen parents will find themselves in a co-parenting relationship with the father or mother of their child where what binds them together is the best interests of their shared child, not their relationship with each other. However, even in best-case scenarios where a child's physical, emotional, spiritual, and educational best interests are met from the perspective of the court and at least one parent, co-parenting can be a contentious and difficult situation when the other parent doesn't agree, or the parents don't get along for personal reasons.

Many teens will not find themselves in long-term relationships with the mother or father of their child. This makes it critical to understand what co-parenting is and to develop a set of mutually agreed upon guidelines of how you are going to interact with each other and raise your child.

One of the reasons it's so hard for parents to work together after a break-up (or divorce in many cases) is because what's in the "best interest" of the child

Fathers Have Rights

Although it may not seem like it at times, fathers have more rights than they realize. Each state's Department of Social Services provides extensive resources to assist fathers. However, many departments across the nation state very clearly that if fathers want to exercise their rights, they need to take the appropriate actions and not wait for the state to step in. "An unmarried father has rights and responsibilities concerning custody, visitation, and child support. However, an unmarried father needs to take legal action to obtain these rights and responsibilities and must sign an Acknowledgement of Paternity form."[f]

isn't clear and can be open to the perspectives of the court, social workers, teen mother, teen father, and even paternal or maternal grandparents. The UN Convention on the Rights of the Child defines *best interests of the child* as "a primary consideration in all actions concerning children, whether undertaken by public or private social welfare institutions, courts of law, administrative authorities or legislative bodies."[18] This basically says that what's best for the child should be top of the mind in any and all actions taken on behalf of that child. But what is "best" is often subjective. Edward Kruk, PhD, specializes in child and family policy and writes that the best approach is to focus on the children's core needs: "I would suggest that when we talk about the 'best interests' of children, we should be primarily concerned with their essential needs, helping children grow and develop, and achieve their capabilities to the maximum extent possible. Needs are the nutriments or conditions essential to a child's growth and integrity, and for every need there is a corresponding responsibility."[19] Thus, co-parenting isn't about who is right and who is wrong. It's not about who is the better or worse parent, and it's not about winning or losing. It's about making decisions together that will help your child's future be healthier, happier, and more stable. Being able to effectively work together as parents has immense benefits for children. Children whose parents cooperate and work together feel more secure, thrive with consistency since they know what's expected of them isn't going to change from one parent to the next, and are able to independently solve problems and reach more positive resolutions.[20]

Getting Past Emotions

Co-parenting requires both parents to drop their emotional baggage when they interact with one another and with their children. Sound impossible? Overcome with rage, anger, distrust, and disgust by the choices your parenting partner has made recently or in the past? Unfortunately, studies and researchers agree that those emotions are only going to make things worse for the kids. Next time you're frustrated or just got off a ridiculous phone call with your ex and are ready to spew, try the following:

- Call up someone you can vent to—but not when the kids are around or within earshot. Friends and family are great sounding boards for your relationship woes. They typically know what you've been through and can help you get through those first few initial feelings of anger and frustration. However, be careful not to vent, talk down, or criticize in front of your kids. This sets a bad example by teaching kids to talk behind someone's back negatively. It can also be unsettling and confusing for kids to hear one parent knock another as they are loyal to and love both. Remember, oftentimes, your child/children didn't experience the problems and issues you had with your ex so they aren't sympathetic and at very young ages can't even understand the emotional context of the issues. It's best to keep your frustrations in check until you can talk and vent in a place without little impressionable ears.
- Get business-like. Take the time to know and understand your custody and parenting agreement rights. It could help to get a free consultation with a lawyer or the court system to better understand or develop, if you don't have one, a co-parenting agreement. Areas like who has the kids when and for how long can be really clear. Other areas—like how to make decisions about activities, who pays for what, day care, and the best way to communicate (phone, text, e-mail) with each other—might get muddy and require formal court-appointed mediation to work through and develop a set of guidelines to live by. Knowing what your rules and boundaries are for the relationship you have with each other and the child can help offset the emotions. Also, treating each other like you would a colleague or work associate—with respect and detachment from his or her personal life—can also help create an environment where you're better able to get along for the sake of your child/children.
- Pick your battles. Major decisions like education, medical care, and the child's financial well-being should be mutually agreed upon. Other decisions, like what sports or groups the child is involved in and what happens

on a dad day versus a mom day, may be outside of your control. If the child is safe and healthy when he or she is with the other parent, the logistics and actual activities he or she engages in may not be any of your business. For example, if you want bedtime to be 7:00 p.m. and your ex consistently puts the kids down around 8:30 p.m., you not only don't have a lot of legal wiggle room to fight that battle, but you also may be picking fights for the wrong reasons. The style in which we raise children is largely individual and letting go can be scary. Try to see your reactions (or overreactions) as your struggling with not having control over every single decision and interaction other people have with your child. Take this knowledge to fight the dread and anxiety you may be feeling by taking a walk, talking to someone you trust, and maybe even trying to understand why your ex is keeping the child/children up later. Sometimes listening to the other side, even if you don't ever agree, can give you a deeper perspective that allows you to better deal with and emotionally handle his or her decisions.

Key Co-parenting Decisions

Not sure where to start? Here are some hot topics to discuss with your ex, either together or through formal mediation, so you both can (hopefully) come up with a parenting plan to avoid any bumps or challenges that will inevitably arise in the future:

- **Medical needs.** Who will be your child's primary care provider? Which parent will hold the insurance and how is the other parent going to get a copy of that information? Is one parent going to be primarily "in charge" or taking the child/children to medical visits and appointments? What is the communication plan for letting the other parent know what's going on after a visit or appointment? Will the child be vaccinated/immunized? What about flu shots?
- **Education.** What school district will the child attend? How is he or she getting to school—bus, taxi, walk, parent, carpool? What school will the child be attending—public, private, or religious? What is the class schedule? What does the after-school care situation look like—is the child bussed to day care, going home with a friend, having a parent or family member pick up? Is one parent going to be a primary contact for the school? How are both parents going to get access to schedules, parent-teacher conferences, and important school events? Does the school have information for both parents? What after-school activities will the child be involved in? What will the process be for sharing report cards and progress

reports—will one parent share with the other, or will the school provide two copies, one for each parent? What will the process be for talking and disciplining the child/children for grades that don't meet expectations or poor behavior at school?

- **Finances.** Who pays for the cost of education, activities, and medical care? Are the costs split between both parents? What are the shared expenses versus individual expenses? If one parent pays, how soon after does the other parent (in the event it's a shared expense) have to pay back his or her share?
- **Rules and consequences.** Obviously, rules aren't going to be the same for both households since each parent is going to parent in accordance with his or her unique style and parenting strategy. However, the more consistent each household is, the more likely the child will feel safe and secure in each when he or she is away from the other. While there are some rules that are going to be specific to each household and each parent should respect those boundaries, rules like grade and homework expectations, curfews, and behaviors and activities that are unacceptable (stealing, lying, and being disrespectful to name a few) can be considered nonnegotiable for each household. By setting up some standard rules, you and your ex can also talk about consequences for breaking those rules that can be adhered to in each household.
- **Schedule.** This is a tricky one and a cause for some discomfort and frustration for parents who want their child's schedule to be identical in each household. Try to talk to your ex about what elements of scheduling you each can mirror with the other. Mealtimes, bedtimes, bathing, how much screen time the child is allowed, and any dietary restrictions are a few topics to discuss in order to make the child's adjustment to having two homes a positive one. It's not about one parent's personal feelings about what's best, but both parents determining what's best in order for the child to feel safe, secure, and loved.
- **Activities.** Will your child be in scouting? Dance? Baseball? Wrestling? Chess club? Will he or she take any music lessons? What about religious or spiritual upbringing? Will both parents commit to taking the child to scheduled activities and games even if he or she isn't personally attached to the activity? Talking about the various enrichment activities, who's taking the child where and on what days, and the level of involvement of each parent in the activity can help parents support the child.

These are just a few of the questions parents can discuss together and potentially agree to in order to improve their ongoing co-parenting relationship and help their child or children adjust and feel stable in a split-household situation.

Investing time, effort, and energy into repairing broken relationships and creating new relationships will ensure teens have the support system and social network they need to thrive as parents and individuals—through good times and bad.

Taking the time, effort, and energy to reestablish lost trust, make new friends or nurture existing friendships, and come up with a plan for working with your partner can be overwhelming. Teen parents may feel like they don't have the energy to spend on their relationships, but putting the extra work into key relationships can provide teens with a better support system and network, which can help

Try This! Get Fiscally Fit

Understanding what's involved from a cost perspective for baby can be a bonding experience for couples . . . but it can also end up a nightmare if couples don't talk at all and assume the other will cover certain expenses. BabyCenter.com has a great suggestion: "Sit down with your partner and/or caregivers to discuss how you'll handle new-baby expenses—clothes, food, diapers, toys, and gear can add up fast. Brainstorm where you can trim your budget to make room for your baby's needs. Consider making some budget adjustments now, and start banking your savings for your baby."[9]

them as they navigate parenthood. Having boundaries and being able to emotionally detach from unhealthy relationships, or aspects of negative relationships, can also free up mental and emotional energy for teens and allow them to focus their thoughts and attention on more positive aspects of their life, like caring for baby, finishing school, and achieving their dreams.

FINISHING SCHOOL

According to the National Campaign to Prevent Teen and Unplanned Pregnancy, parenthood is the leading reason why teen girls drop out of school. Less than half of teen mothers ever graduate from high school and fewer than 2 percent earn a college degree by age thirty.[1] However, many teen mothers and fathers do finish high school successfully and go on to earn college and graduate degrees. But how, in the face of so many challenges, do they do it? How can teens raise a child while finishing high school and then attending college? What if they don't have anywhere for the child to go; how do they find child care? What if they don't even know what they want to do in college in the first place?

Every person, especially parents raising a family and thinking about going back to school, asks him- or herself these questions—even men and woman who are going back when they are much older. Part of being a responsible parent is understanding what your role as a parent is. What are the key things you have to provide to your child? What kind of life do you want your child to have? Are you currently in a position to provide that kind of life? How are you going to do that if you're not?

Many teens, overwhelmed by the amount of responsibility that comes with having and raising a child, drop out of high school with the mind-set they will

---

! Try This! Develop Your Parenting Strategy

• Take some time to think about what kind of parent you want to be and what kind of co-parenting relationship you want with your partner. BabyCenter. com suggests the following: "To get the conversation going, try this creative writing exercise: Each of you makes two lists, one titled 'My mother always . . .' and one titled 'My mother never . . .' Then do the same for 'My father always/ My father never.' When you're done, talk about what you wrote down and decide together which behaviors you value and which you'd like to change as you raise your child." Is your partner not involved? Still consider doing the exercise and get an idea for your own parenting desires and philosophies.[a]

Nausea, sleepless nights, and feeling like they don't fit in or have the time to deal with school while raising a baby are a few of the many reasons teens drop out. However, there are many nontraditional options available to teen parents to ensure they finish high school and even go on to pursue advanced degrees.

finish once their child is older and they have a better grip on being a parent. As the stats indicate, most dropouts fail to ever finish.

Postsecondary Education

Life without a high school education is grim. Dropouts commit about 75 percent of crimes in the United States;[2] earn $200,000 less than a high school graduate over a lifetime and almost a million dollars less than a college graduate;[3] and are less healthy and more prone to illness, depression, and even losing their teeth.[4] For those teens who think they can just skip high school and jump right to college . . . think again. Most postsecondary educational institutions won't accept applicants without a high school diploma, GED (General Educational Development), or state equivalent. In the event they do, applicants are typically required to take additional placement tests in order for the institution to understand which courses best fit the applicant's experience, current education, and career goals. If applicants do not even meet basic class requirements based on their test scores, they may be required to earn a GED, or what the state considers equivalent to a

GED, before they can move forward and actually take classes. Dropouts may also have to fund their education largely on their own or find an institution willing to provide grants or scholarships since individuals without a diploma or GED are not eligible for federal student aid.

While a high school education will be invaluable to teen parents and will open doors for them since having a GED or diploma meets most entry-level basic job qualifications and college entry requirements, it's still incredibly hard to get ahead with just a high school education.

This is why ongoing education—whether college, university, technical school, apprenticeship, or certification—is crucial. But because they are teens, and many teens aren't sure what they want to go to college for or "what they want to be when they grow up," teen parents have a bit more than just raising a child to work against them. They have very typical teen angst about not knowing what to do. However, having a baby and family to support can provide teen parents with added motivation to dig deep within themselves and figure out what the best post–high school education is for them.

Following are general overviews for some of the major types of institutions available throughout the United States. Each type of educational institution provides different benefits and programs from a traditional classroom setting to a more nontraditional online environment. Getting a feel for the type of institution and the types of programs and degrees offered at each can help teens decide what next steps to take in their educational and career journey.

Vocational, Technical, Business, and Trade Schools

Vocational, technical, business, and trade schools offer programs that focus on real-world job training. Most of the programs offered prepare graduates for careers within a relatively short amount of time, usually a few months to two years. Since these schools focus on preparing graduates for careers in two years or less, the types of programs offered typically hone in on a particular field or skill. What follows is just a small list of the types of programs trade schools generally offer. However, doing an Internet search for "vocational, trade, or technical schools" in your city or state can yield specific schools and programs along with their requirements for admission. Another great benefit of these types of institutions is they tend to be flexible and offer night, weekend, and online courses.

- Business degrees such as management, administration, marketing, and accounting
- Construction management
- Cosmetology and nail technician programs

- Creative programs such as graphic design, digital entertainment design, floral design, and interior design
- Criminal justice programs that prepare graduates to become police officers
- Electronics installation and maintenance
- Health care programs to prepare graduates to become nurses, transcriptionists, certified nursing assistants, dental assistants and hygienists, and more
- Hotel and restaurant management
- Paralegal training programs
- Technology-focused programs such as information systems, project management, programming, and software development
- Trade-focused programs such as welding, plumbing, carpentry, drafting, automotive repair, and even truck-driving training

Two-Year Community or Junior Colleges

These educational institutions are very similar to traditional four-year colleges and universities with a few exceptions. Unlike the rigorous application process of traditional colleges and universities, most two-year colleges only require a high school diploma, GED, or state equivalent for enrollment. One of the biggest advantages graduates and students cite for enrolling in a two-year college is that these types of educational institutions usually offer full credit for the first two years of a college or university education and guaranteed transferability, but at a much lower cost than four-year schools. Many junior colleges cost less than $2,000 each semester to attend full time. Due to the lower cost of tuition, community colleges can be a great way for students who aren't sure what they want to do long term to take a variety of interesting classes with highly qualified professors and flexible schedules to better determine what career they're most interested in pursuing. However, those looking for a bustling campus life and a really diverse and wide variety of courses may find junior and community colleges lacking. While they are less expensive and offer flexible class schedules students can build around their work and home lives, two-year colleges may not have the same amount of clubs, athletics, and organizations available for students to get involved in.

Four-Year Colleges and Universities

Unlike two-year colleges and trade schools, four-year colleges and universities are less vocationally based and feature a broader curriculum. What does this mean? It means students are required to take various courses like fine arts, literature, technology, math, philosophy, and other core classes that aren't necessarily part of

Financial Aid

Are you determined to advance your educational goals, but worried about how you're going to pay for them? Check out the office of Federal Student Aid. As a part of the U.S. Department of Education, the Federal Student Aid office is responsible for managing the student financial assistance programs authorized under Title IV of the Higher Education Act of 1965. It offers programs that provide grants, loans, and work-study funds to students attending college or career school. You may be eligible for some kind of assistance, support, or loan to help achieve your dreams and goals. Go to the free application for Federal Student Aid (https://fafsa.ed.gov/) and learn about the different types of programs, how to apply, and how to get in contact with one of the representatives.

their degree, but the college or university feels are imperative to a well-rounded education. Typically, the first two years of a four-year degree will be primarily composed of general requirements and electives. The main benefit of a four-year college? According to author Christina Couch in her comparison of two-year versus four-year colleges, "Four-year institutions offer an enormous spectrum of on- and off-campus learning opportunities. On campus you can attend performances, cultural events, and guest lecture series, as well as participate in student-run clubs and honor societies. Students also go off campus for service-learning projects, study abroad trips, internships, cooperative education programs, and field trips."[5] Four-year colleges and universities also come at a hefty price. According to the College Board, the average cost of tuition and fees for the 2014–2015 school year for four-year colleges was $31,231 at private colleges; $9,139 for state residents at public colleges; and $22,958 for out-of-state residents attending public universities.[6] Tuition and fees for the 2014–2015 school year for two-year colleges came in at $3,347.[7]

At the end of the day, what postsecondary educational steps teen parents choose to make will be largely personal. It could be a dream to attend a four-year traditional program and major in journalism, go premed, or study economics regardless of the investment. Whatever your decision, a postsecondary education will improve your lifestyle, opportunities, and economic situation.

In Her Words: Q&A with Teen Mom Holly

Holly is a single teen mother of one who is working to achieve her educational and career goals.

Growing up, Holly lived with her parents and brother. Her dad, an RN, struggled with prescription substance abuse and alcohol. She found out later that he went to rehab when she was about in third grade, but that he started using again after his mom passed away. When Holly was in seventh grade, her dad went to the doctor and found out he had stage four colon cancer. He passed away her sophomore year in high school. Her mom tried to keep a happy facade for Holly and her brother, but it didn't help Holly. "The problem with the whole family situation was I understood what was going on with my dad. To this day, my brother has a facade of my dad. My brother will always look up to him." The family even took part in therapy for three years of high school, and while each did take away positive coping tools, it was a heartbreaking process because everyone in the family was suffering the loss and trying to deal with it in his and her own way. "There was fighting, screaming, and yelling. Everyone was selfish. I wanted everyone to understand what I was going through. My mom didn't think people understood her," said Holly.[b]

The tremendous loss of her father and the stress it placed on her family is when Holly's problems started. She started drinking heavily; doing marijuana and pain killers she got from her boyfriend, who was a year older; and partying to cope with the loss of her father and the family as she had known it.

Holly sat down with me to share her story in hopes that other teen parents will find inspiration and hope in her experiences and go on to be better people and parents.

Author Jessica Akin (JA): How old were you when you first started having sex?

Holly Hagaman (HH): We were both fifteen and sober. We didn't know what we were doing because it was his first time too. It wasn't what you think it would be like. I thought it was going to be like in a movie—rolling around in bed together. It was painful and not fun. We had planned it. We had talked about it and went to the store and bought condoms. After, I felt bad. I couldn't believe. My first reaction was "he's going to leave me."[c]

JA: Did you talk about birth control?

HH: Pregnancy was the first thing that came up when we talked about it. We were doing everything to prevent it. I wasn't really open to the idea of abortion, but we were having sex for three months and we got pregnant. I didn't tell my mom, but my mom had a feeling and made me take a test. My mom told my dad. He was upset. I struggled with the fact my daughter will never have a grandpa and I felt guilty that the first baby would have known my dad. He would have been a great grandpa. My mom was devastated, but she told me that the decision to keep the baby was up to me. When we came to the decision and I thought it was best, she was supportive and came with me. She stayed home with me. I was scared and had an abortion at fifteen. I felt bad for years, but realized there's nothing I can do about it now.

The experience of having an abortion was awful. I took the pill and remember sitting in the bathroom with a bucket puking and bleeding clumps the size of oranges. All day. Sick as a dog. You have to eat before and I ate buttered noodles and that was all I could taste the rest of the day. It was terrible. The whole time you're sitting there and questioning if it was the right decision. To say I don't feel guilty isn't true. But at that time, it was the only decision I could have made. I also believe that if I hadn't done it, I wouldn't have had Emmy. I wouldn't have the life I have now. A life that I want.

So my boyfriend's family wanted me to keep the baby. His mom didn't allow me in their house and called me all types of names. He didn't really care one way or another if I kept it. He was cheating on me with multiple people. Two weeks before my dad died, my dad told me to leave him. That he wasn't good for me. After he told me that, I broke up with him.

JA: Tell me about the hobbies, interests, and friends you had before you got pregnant. Has any of that changed?

HH: Singing. I sang in the Milwaukee Children's Choir for five years. In middle school and high school I played softball. I played rugby in high school too. I did all the plays at my middle school. I was the evil stepmom in Cinderella. It kept me busy. Rugby was perfect—it was my go-to after school to go beat everyone up.

Now, is laundry and cleaning a hobby? Sleeping? I've been waitressing for three years. I like working. For fun now, I play with my daughter. I spend all my time with her. I take her everywhere with me. Every once in a while, I go out once every few months to the bars or do something fun. Emmy will go to my mom's for a sleepover.

I scrapbook all the time. I love doing that. Emmy's scrapbook is huge. If you would have asked me this three years ago, I would have told you I had a ton more going on.

JA: What are your career goals? How did you finish high school? What was your experience like?

HH: I graduated high school. I was eighteen when I got pregnant and nineteen when I had her. Senior year of high school I didn't care and didn't go to class. My mom would ride my ass to go to school, but as a parent, she didn't know what to do.

If someone would have told me in high school that I needed a B−, I would have done it. I was just striving to pass with a D. I would have busted it one hundred times more and made an effort. If I knew I need to push it more . . . I would have.

I enrolled at MATC [Milwaukee Area Technical College in Wisconsin] and want to go into Labor and Delivery as an RN.

JA: What is your support system like?

HH: I did live at home and moved out in November 2014. I like it. My boyfriend, my daughter, and I live in an upper duplex. My daughter has her own room and it's decorated really pretty.

My mom was amazing and let us live with her. She even switched bedrooms so my daughter and I could be upstairs with the master bedroom and our own bathroom. We had our own space. But the whole time I was there, I felt like a burden and we were taking over. When my brother would have friends over, I felt bad telling them to be quiet because the baby was sleeping. My mom also used to have a lot of friends, but after I had Emmy, they all stopped asking her to hang out. And my mom is doing so much since I moved out. She stopped putting her life on hold, which makes me happy because I can see her doing more.

My boyfriend is really focused and driven for the future. He is going to school for business finance. He is going to a private university and he got a football scholarship, but felt that the culture wasn't in synch with his values and transferred to a community college. He works hard, forty hours a week, and takes odd jobs trying to save money and build a future for our family.

JA: Tell me about your dreams—what are you working toward?

HH: Going back to school and we'd like to buy a house eventually. We live within our means. It's not that we have a budget, but if we don't have the money, we won't do it. Every paycheck, we put ten dollars in a jar and ten dollars in Emmy's bank account. The jar is our fun money to go out to dinner or vacation.

Eventually, my boyfriend and I would like to get married and have our own kids, but we want to wait to get married to have more kids. I was engaged to Emmy's dad; he proposed when we got pregnant. I feel like if we have a baby outside of wedlock, he might just leave. With Emmy's dad, it was easy for him to go. Now, I want to be married because that is truly a commitment, you make a vow to stand by each other. But for today, we want to be financially stable. A majority of having a baby is financial.

Beating the Odds

Teen parents raising a family are going to face almost insurmountable odds to finish school. Pregnant teens may feel embarrassed, new babies may have hard-to-care-for conditions or illnesses that keep parents away from their educational responsibilities, day care may be difficult to find or unaffordable, teens may have to work during the hours in which they'd be attending classes, and teens may not have any family or friends to help them get through the stress and additional burden of taking care of an infant and studying for exams. These are only a few examples of the many obstacles new parents and teen parents may face on a day-to-day basis. But they are simply that—obstacles not impossibles. Teens who realize they will have to overcome these challenges and look for solutions will be better equipped to succeed.

This will take research on their part. Many teens may not be aware of the many programs offered in their communities. Do some online research and call around to get more information on online, homeschool, or traditional high school or GED programs designed for pregnant teens and teen parents; look into high schools and colleges with on-site day care centers; and check out local day care centers or private in-home providers. Many colleges are now offering online and night school programs. Find out which ones are in your area and budget. While the initial requirements posted online or in a brochure may seem to preclude teens from being part of those programs, calling and explaining your situation to an admissions counselor can help him or her understand your unique needs and make an exception so that you can enroll and pursue your education. However, it will take time and effort to not only learn what program best fits your situation, but also how you can best ensure your own success. Finding a flexible job to pay for college and potentially day care, applying for as many grants and scholarships as possible, and taking out student loans on top of missing some time with your child and forgoing the parties and a social life may be short-term sacrifices to ensure the long-term happiness of yourself and your family.

Thoughts on Child Care

Finding quality, trustworthy, and dependable child care, either at school, with family members, through a private in-home sitter, or through a church or community group such as the YMCA can make or break any parent's success in achieving their career or educational goals. Not to mention his or her peace of mind! It's never easy leaving a child with someone other than yourself, and this isn't an issue specific to teen parents—all parents struggle and many feel that finding the perfect sitter or center to care for their child is among the most important decisions they make. Here are only a few questions you can ask. Start your search early and tailor your list of questions to best fit your personality and needs:

- How long have you been in business? Do you meet state licensing requirements? If a day care center: Does the center meet any accreditations or are you part of any affiliations or memberships? Providers that are accredited have met voluntary standards for child care that are higher than most state licensing requirements. The National Association for the Education of Young Children and the National Association for Family Child Care are the two largest organizations that accredit child care programs.
- What is your adult to child ratio? Babies need an adult to child ratio of no more than 1:4 (one adult for four infants), while four-year-olds can do well with a ratio of 1:10 (one adult for ten children).

- What are your qualifications for caregivers? Are they college educated? Do they all meet licensing requirements? Are they required to take ongoing education to stay current on child development needs and milestones?
- What is the turnover rate for caregivers—do they stick around or does the center have an issue keeping quality caregivers? Are all the caregivers CPR trained and certified?
- How do caretakers discipline or deal with bad behavior? What about rewarding good behavior?
- When does the center or caretaker open? How early can you pick up? How late can you drop off?
- Are there closures for holidays, events, or vacations? How much notice will you receive in advance of closures?
- Do I have to adhere to a predetermined, set schedule or do I pay as I go? Is there a late-pick-up fee? Do I pay if my child is ill or on vacation?
- Are snacks or meals included in the fees? What supplies do I need to provide?
- Are parent visits encouraged? Be strongly cautioned if they are not or if the provider seems annoyed that you'd ask to pop in. In fact, it's best even if you love your provider, to randomly stop by to check in or even pick your child up early to ensure all is well. It should never be a problem! The well-being of your child should always be your primary concern—not worrying about making a child care provider angry or annoyed by stopping.
- How will you (the center or caretakers) communicate with me? Texts, e-mails, newsletters, and/or phone calls? Will I receive updates on my child's behavior?
- What activities are done with the children? Is there a formal curriculum or educational structure? If there is, ask for a copy or a copy of their weekly/monthly schedule of activities. Check out the indoor and outdoor play areas to ensure there are age-appropriate options for your child.
- What are your policies for hygiene and sanitation? How often are the toys and the center cleaned? Make sure the center, facility, or home is clean and has all appropriate safety measures in place. If anything seems dingy or unkempt, you may want to keep looking to find a better fit.
- Do all of your caretakers follow a similar feeding and sleeping schedule? What is your policy for TV watching? How will your providers discipline my child? Are there opportunities for active physical play as well as more quiet activities? How do your caretakers support infant, toddler, and preschool-age children's social, emotional, and intellectual development? Check out how the caregivers interact with the other children. Make sure the other children seem happy and well cared for and that you get good feeling and vibe from the place.

Teens who make a decision to finish high school and then go on to obtain postsecondary degrees report they are happier, more financially successful, and better able to care for their children.

- For a day care center: Can I get involved by volunteering for field trips or activities?
- Can I speak to parents who would be willing to provide a referral?

Want more support? Contact Child Care Aware's Child Care Resource and Referral agency. Representatives will help you find providers in your area: 1-800-424-2246. The representatives can also help you understand what the licensing requirements are where you live, how to get information about any complaints and violations, and if you qualify for any child care financial assistance.

Try This! Install the Car Seat

Your baby can't come home with you unless you have an infant car seat and it's installed correctly. Review the car seat manual for installation instructions or get some help from a car seat safety inspector. Not sure where to find one? Go to http://cert.safekids.org/ and find someone who can help.

Finishing high school and pursing postsecondary education is possible for teen parents, but it's not easy. It will require grit and determination. It will also require making a plan for how you're going to get to and from school and child care, and how you'll pay for school and child care. By planning ahead and being committed to your education, you'll absolutely improve your future and the future of your child.

HEALTH RISKS AND COMPLICATIONS

Although from a biological and physiological standpoint teens are as likely as older women to deliver healthy babies, teens and their babies still undergo physical and emotional risks and complications that are unique to their age demographic. In a report prepared by the National Campaign to Prevent Teen Pregnancy, it was found that teen mothers are more likely to deliver prematurely and to have low-birth-weight babies, with accompanying risks of infant death, blindness, deafness, retardation, mental illness, and other permanent problems. Babies born to teens are also less likely to survive their first year than those born to mothers in their twenties and thirties, and 14 percent of all teen pregnancies also end in miscarriage.[1]

One of the major reasons cited by research and health care professionals for this disparity between teens and older women is that teens are least likely of all maternal age groups to get early and regular prenatal care, and many teens need to improve their lifestyles in order to increase their odds of having a healthy baby.[2] This chapter will outline the risks and potential complications often found in teen pregnancies and offer resources on how to mitigate them so that teens can ensure a healthy pregnancy and birth.

Try This! Stock Up

Take some time to determine what you need to have on hand at home in order to be better prepared for baby's arrival and reduce the need for you to run around at the last minute. Essentials like diapers, wipes, bottles, formula, a thermometer, pacifiers, baby soap and lotions, and swaddling blankets are givens to have on hand. Some moms also suggest making several meals in advance and freezing them and having extra paper towels, shampoo, conditioner, toothpaste, soap, dishwashing soap, and laundry detergent stocked up.

```
24/24▯    09:37:43
26Hz    5.0M S-H
        DVA: 100%
        GA:30w2d

                        +AC
                          27.3cm
                        31w3d±21d
                        09.21,'01
                        pl-avg( 2)
                        31w3d±21d
                        09.21,'01

            R17 G90 C3
MEASUREMENT    1        2        3        4        5        6
B-1          Data,  DIST.   BPD      HC       AC       Next
             Clear         Hadlock  Hadlock  Hadlock   Page
```

Teen mothers can reduce the probability of delivering early, having low-birth-weight babies, and experiencing preeclampsia by practicing good prenatal care and seeing their obstetric provider on a regular basis.

Risks and Concerns

A teenage mother is at greater risk than women over age twenty for pregnancy complications, such as premature labor, anemia, low birth weight, and preeclampsia (high blood pressure). These risks are even greater for teens who are under fifteen years old.[3]

Preeclampsia

Preeclampsia is a medical condition where a woman's blood pressure is elevated to unhealthy levels, and there may be protein found in the urine or other issues with the liver and kidneys during pregnancy. While preeclampsia affects only about 5 percent of women, pregnant teens are at an increased risk. Preeclampsia causes blood vessels to constrict, which is why blood pressure increases, and this constricting reduces the blood flow to a pregnant woman's liver, kidneys, and brain.

Symptoms typically start after twenty weeks of pregnancy and while they vary from woman to woman, they can include severe or persistent headaches, sudden issues with vision, pain or tenderness in the upper abdomen, nausea, and vomiting. The only cure for preeclampsia is delivering the baby, so the best method of detection and prevention is attending all prenatal visits. This way, your obstetrics health care provider can check urine samples and screen for other preeclampsia related symptoms and come up with a treatment plan that best fits your situation.[4]

Premature Labor

Babies are considered full term at forty weeks, and research shows that being pregnant for at least thirty-nine weeks allows babies to grow and develop fully. Although any woman can deliver a baby preterm—even if she has no risk factors—more babies are born preterm, or before thirty-seven weeks, to teens and women forty and older than any other maternal age group.[5] Babies born preterm, "preemies," can face very serious health issues. Preemies have higher rates of health complications and lifelong disabilities, including mental retardation, learning and behavioral problems, cerebral palsy, lung problems, vision and hearing loss, diabetes, high blood pressure, and heart disease.[6] In the event you feel any labor pains, call your health care professional immediately. In some cases, premature labor can be stopped with certain medications or bed rest.

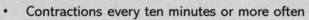

Signs of Preterm Labor

If you are experiencing any of these signs, please call your health care professional immediately:

- Contractions every ten minutes or more often
- Change in vaginal discharge
- Pelvic pressure
- Low, dull backache
- Cramps that feel like your period
- Abdominal cramps with or without diarrhea[a]

Low Birth Weight

Teens are also at higher risk of having babies with low birth weight, and this can be attributed to the fact teens have a higher risk of delivering earlier. The sooner a baby is delivered, the smaller and less developed it is likely to be. A baby is considered "low birth weight" when it weighs only 3.3 to 5.5 pounds and "very low birth weight" when it weighs less than 3.3 pounds.[7] Babies this small often require extra, highly specialized care after birth, and because of this, are often admitted to a hospital's neonatal care unit to help with any risks that typically arise from low birth weights and underdevelopment, for example, breathing problems, brain or spine issues, heart conditions, gut and digestive disorders, eye problems, jaundice, anemia, and infections. Depending on how early you deliver and the health problems the baby experiences, the baby's hospital stay can range from a few hours to several weeks and even months in the neonatal unit before going home.

Miscarriage

The loss of a pregnancy can be overwhelming, shocking, and depressing even when it was unplanned, unexpected, and maybe even unwanted at first. Teens who experience the loss of a pregnancy, whether through miscarriage, stillbirth, or another condition, usually go on to have healthy pregnancies later in life. However, dealing with the emotional toll and grief is not easy. While teens can experience a stillbirth or pregnancy loss through other conditions, this section focuses just on miscarriage since it is considered one of the top risks associated with teen pregnancies. There are many resources available to help support teens dealing with such a painful and heartbreaking loss, and several are included in chapter 10.

> "i never got to hold you. i never got to tell you i loved you. i never got to hold your hand. i never got to show you a daisy. you never saw the sunshine. you never saw my face. you never felt my kisses. you never felt my embrace. you never got to hear me sing to you. i never got to hear you giggle. i never got to watch you sleep. i never got to show you to your daddy. you never got to wake up. you never got to breathe, you never got to live. i miss you. i miss the things we should be sharing right now."—"Poem," by Hannah[b]

Every child-bearing female is at risk for miscarriage regardless of her age. A pregnancy that ends within the first twenty weeks is considered a spontaneous abortion, or miscarriage. About 10 to 20 percent of known pregnancies end in miscarriage, and more than 80 percent of these losses happen before twelve weeks.[8] Sadly, and while the statistics vary, they show anywhere from 10 to 25 percent of teen pregnancies end in miscarriage.[9] According to March of Dimes, possible causes of miscarriage include the following:

- Chromosome problems. This is the cause of more than half of miscarriages that happen in the first trimester.
- Blighted ovum. This is when a fertilized egg implants in the uterus but doesn't develop into a baby and is sometimes caused by chromosome problems.
- Smoking, alcohol, and drugs.
- Mom's health. Hormone problems or infections and health conditions like diabetes, thyroid disease, and lupus may increase a woman's chances for having a miscarriage. Being up front and sharing any health issues or concerns with your obstetrics health care provider can help them create a treatment and prenatal plan that supports your pregnancy and helps mitigate the risk of miscarriage.[10]

The rate of miscarriage is thought to be higher among teens due to the fact teens are still growing and developing themselves, and their diets and lifestyles either lack key nutrients or include variables like smoking, drinking, and drug use that can harm a developing baby.

Contact your health care provider if you are experiencing any of the following symptoms:

- Strong cramps that make you double over or make it hard to catch your breath
- White or pink mucus-like discharge
- Discharge that includes tissue resembling blood clots
- Labor-like contractions

"While i was away in spain i told my brothers girlfriend about bump.
She thinks its for the best because of my age. shes wrong.
I cried a lot about bump. It still hard."—Shona[c]

- Heavy bleeding that soaks through a pad in a few hours or less, even without cramps
- Sudden decrease in pregnancy symptoms

Physical recovery times vary from woman to woman and typically take a few weeks to a month or more.[11] Most women get their period again four to six weeks after a miscarriage.[12]

Every parent, whether male or female, copes with the loss of a pregnancy differently. Some parents try for another child right away, while others need time to understand and process their feelings. Some benefit and heal from the support of friends, family, and a community or network of other individuals who have experienced a similar loss. Yet others need alone time and stay away from friends and family for a while until they are in a better place emotionally. However, if your feelings of grief seem to linger and continually drag you down, let your health care provider know. He or she will have resources and connections with therapists and other providers who can provide additional support and help as you work through your emotions and sadness.

Take Ownership for Your Health: Prenatal Care

Unfortunately, the biggest issues aren't risks specifically attributed to pregnancy, but rather the choices a teen mom makes in the course of her day that can harm her and the baby. Teens are 33 percent more likely to smoke than women in their twenties and thirties who are pregnant and twice as likely not to receive any prenatal care. These behaviors lead to their unknowingly and unintentionally putting their baby's health and life on the line. Pregnant teens who don't have supportive parents or a network of friends and family to help them are at an even more increased risk for not getting adequate medical care.[13]

How Often Do I Have to Go?

To help you plan and prepare for prenatal care visits, it helps to understand the frequency in which you'll see your health care provider. For a healthy and complication-free pregnancy, most health care providers will want to see you

- every four weeks until the twenty-eighth week of pregnancy;
- then every two weeks until the thirty-sixth week; and finally
- once a week until your big day—the delivery!

Prenatal care is absolutely the most important priority pregnant teens should have, especially in the first few months. But what is prenatal care?

Prenatal care is typically administered by your health care obstetrics provider, so the information in this chapter isn't meant to replace an actual obstetrics provider, but simply clarify what *prenatal care* means and why it's so important to your health and the health of your baby. Also, many of the risks and complications associated with teen pregnancy can be mitigated with good prenatal care, helping you take control over the health and wellness of yourself and your child.

Prenatal care also involves how you take care of yourself during your pregnancy. It includes visits to an obstetrics health care provider for a physical exam, weight check, and urine sample analysis. Some visits may also include lab work for blood samples and also ultrasound exams. The visits allow your health care provider and you to stay aware of any issues impacting your health and the baby's health, and to answer any questions you may have about the pregnancy.

Prenatal Testing and Screening

Prenatal testing typically takes place during the first, second, and third trimesters to help health care providers get a clear picture of mom and baby's overall health. This information allows your doctor or health care provider to tailor a prenatal care plan specifically to mom to best support baby's growth and development. Some of the tests, or screens as they are often referred to, can include

- checking mom's blood type and
- determining if mom has any health conditions like diabetes, anemia, or immunity to certain diseases, or any sexually transmitted diseases.

The tests aren't meant to cast blame or judgment on mom, but instead to detect and reduce any problems like birth defects or abnormalities. They also show exciting aspects like how big the baby is, where the baby is in the uterus, and even the gender!

Prenatal Care Guidelines

During the visits, your provider will give you an idea of what you can do to ensure good prenatal care on your side. These guidelines may seem basic, but consistently following them will ensure a better birth and delivery.

Eat a Balanced, Healthy Diet

Eat lots of vegetables, protein, good fats like avocados and olive oil, and fruits. Try and stay away from any processed foods or highly refined foods like candy, cookies, breads, and starches. The Mayo Clinic advises pregnant women to eat more foods containing key nutrients needed to support the development of baby's brain, bones, and teeth—for example, folate and folic acid found in leafy green vegetables, citrus fruit, and dried beans; calcium found in dairy foods and vegetables like broccoli and kale; and iron and Vitamin D found in animal products like meat, fish, and eggs.[14] Foods high in fiber are also recommended for pregnant women because they aide in digestion. These include most beans and peas, whole grains, nuts, berries, and other fruits and vegetables.

Nix the Smoking, Drinking, and Drugs

Contrary to what you may hear from well-meaning friends and family, there is no "safe" amount of cigarettes, alcohol, or drugs. What you ingest or inhale directly impacts your baby as you share the same body, blood, and nutrients during pregnancy. Smoking decreases the amount of oxygen baby receives while increasing baby's heart rate and chances of miscarriage, still birth, low birth weight, respiratory problems, birth defects, and sudden infant death syndrome.[15] In addition to the risks smoking while pregnant has on baby, drinking alcohol can cause permanent and lifelong harm, including the increased risks of birth defects, hearing problems, intellectual disabilities, learning and behavioral problems, sleeping and sucking problems, and speech and language delays.[16] Drugs like cocaine, ecstasy, heroin, and marijuana and many prescription drugs can increase risks of preterm labor, miscarriage, stillbirth, low birth weight, and birth defects.[17] Drug use can also increase the risk of infections like hepatitis C and HIV to mom and baby and also cause neonatal abstinence syndrome, which is a group of health issues that causes the baby to get addicted to a drug before birth and then have to go through terrible withdrawals after birth.[18] The single best way to make sure your baby is healthy? Stay away from this stuff and only take medications that are recommended and prescribed by your obstetrics health care professional. If you stay away from smoking, alcohol, and drugs, your baby can't possibly be at risk for any smoking-, alcohol-, or drug-related risks, disabilities, or problems.

Take a Daily Prenatal Vitamin

Prenatal vitamins are an essential part of your prenatal care because even those following the best diet can miss vitamins and minerals key to baby's growth and development. They are different than a typical multivitamin because they provide the recommended doses of folic acid, which help prevent neural tube defects in baby; iron, which helps support baby's growth and prevents anemia in mom; and omega-3 fatty acids, which promote baby's brain development. Although many health care centers can provide samples, teens don't need a prescription to get them and almost all prenatal vitamins can be purchased over the counter and come in many forms like chewable, gummy, and gel capped, depending on the brand. Prenatal vitamins shouldn't replace a healthy diet and won't make up for

Addiction Resources

First and foremost, if you are struggling with an addiction to cigarettes, alcohol, or drugs, let your health care provider know right away. He or she can help you figure out the right treatment plan and make sure you have the support to quit. You can also contact many national organizations directly to receive free resources and connect with people in your area who can help. You aren't alone in your addiction and don't have to quit alone.

- Alcoholics Anonymous at www.aa.org or call 1-212-870-3400
- National Council on Alcoholism and Drug Dependence at ncadd.org or call 1-800-622-2255
- National Tobacco Cessation Collaborative at www.tobacco-cessation.org
- Smoking Cessation Support at smokefree.gov/ or call 1-800-Quit-Now
- Substance Abuse Treatment Facility Locator at findtreatment.samhsa.gov or call 1-800-662-4357

a poor diet. They are meant to fill in where a person's diet may come up short on the key nutrients needed to support mom and baby during pregnancy.

Other Things to Consider While Pregnant

In addition to understanding what prenatal care entails, some teens wonder if dying or highlighting hair, tanning, playing sports, getting a tattoo or piercing, and taking prescription or over-the-counter medicines (including aspirin and laxatives) are healthy for baby. They may be surprised that some things are safer than they think (and some things are far more dangerous!).

Dying and Highlighting Hair

There's not a lot of research out there supporting how safe it is to dye your hair while pregnant. The Organization of Teratology Information Services provides information on potential reproductive risks and states there are no reports of hair dye causing changes in human pregnancies and that very little of the chemicals in hair dye are actually absorbed into your system. That being said, BabyCenter.com suggests waiting until the second trimester to color hair when the baby is more developed and less vulnerable. BabyCenter.com also suggests for moms to try highlighting or streaking as opposed to all-over color to reduce the changes of the chemicals coming into contact with the scalp.[19] While the chemicals may pose little risk to the pregnancy overall, the smell may irritate moms and make them nauseous and more uncomfortable than anything!

Teen-2-Teen Education Series

The March of Dimes offers a teen-focused series of videos and curriculum called Teen-2-Teen to teach teens how to make healthy decisions for their own benefit now and for the benefit of any children they may have in the future. The series covers a variety of topics such as the consequences of smoking, alcohol, and drugs; eating right; dealing with peer pressure and stress; and thinking ahead. Teens who go through the program can become peer educators and even lead the program for other groups of teen parents or teen parents-to-be. Check it out at www.marchofdimes.org/volunteers/teen-2-teen.aspx.

Tanning

Tanning is notoriously *not* recommended for anyone due to the health risks and higher-than-normal propensity for those who tan regularly to get skin cancer. So it should come as no surprise that experts don't promote tanning and, instead, promote wearing sunscreen of at least SPF 30 and staying in the shade when outside. Stacey Stapleton from American Baby Team offers great insight: "Pregnant women are especially sensitive to the sun, and too much exposure can cause or worsen skin discoloration (called melasma) that many moms-to-be are already prone to." She also writes that pregnant women are more likely to become dehydrated, so lots of sun time should be avoided, and if they are in the sun, pregnant women should drink plenty of water.[20]

Playing Sports

Exercise has many health benefits for mom and baby, and in most cases, teens won't have to stop participating in the athletic activities they love. However, there are some precautions to take as a pregnant woman. First and foremost, be sure to share your physical fitness level and what sports you play with your health care professional—he or she can tell for sure if a certain activity is safe and sensible. Then, be smart. If you feel exhausted, woozy, shaky, or just not yourself while playing, it's time for a time-out. Also, stay away from sports that are highly physical, like rugby or basketball, or can cause you to fall or get hurt, like Rollerblading, downhill skiing, and horseback riding. Check with your health care provider, but Better Health Channel provides some simple rules to follow as a start:

Try This! Move It

● Activity and exercise can make you feel better and improve your pregnancy experience. From taking a stroll around the block to taking a class at your local YMCA or community center, there are many options out there for teens. It's great for your health during and after pregnancy as well according to BabyCenter.com: "If you haven't already, now is a good time to start a regular workout. Joining a class can help motivate you to stick with it. And many women find that prenatal exercise classes are a wonderful way to bond with and get support from other pregnant women. Some good options include water exercise, prenatal yoga or Pilates, a walking group, or a dance class designed for pregnant women."[d]

- Avoid raising your body temperature too high—for example, don't soak in hot spas or exercise to the point of heavy sweating. Reduce your level of exercise on hot or humid days.
- Don't exercise to the point of exhaustion.
- If weight training, choose low weights and medium to high repetitions.
- Avoid exercise if you are ill or feverish.
- Don't increase the intensity of your sporting program while you are pregnant, and always work at less than 75 percent of your maximum heart rate.
- Listen to your body. If you feel weak, experience bleeding or spotting, or experience anything that doesn't seem "normal" for your pregnancy, call your health care provider immediately.[21]

Tattoos and Piercings

This is another area that doesn't have a lot of research to support or recommend against it—which should be telling because that means there's not a lot of information out there about what's in the tattoo dye and if it harms the baby! One of the biggest concerns tattoos raise is around the transfer of diseases like hepatitis B and HIV from the needles used. The American Pregnancy Association suggests waiting until after the baby comes and after moms are done breastfeeding to get a tattoo since it is possible the chemicals in the dye could harm the baby. There is also the risk that a hospital won't administer an epidural if you have a new back tattoo.[22] Although the American Pregnancy Association leaves the decision to get a tattoo largely up to the woman because the risks aren't very clear, when it comes to piercings, they issue a very direct and poignant caution: "A word of warning: Women are encouraged not to have piercings done on the belly button, nipples or genitalia during pregnancy or while trying to conceive because of the physical changes happening in your body at this time. As your breasts and stomach grow, the holes do not completely heal and often become larger and more susceptible to infection. Women should avoid piercing the belly and nipples during pregnancy."[23]

Over-the-Counter Medications

As mentioned earlier, all medications and prescriptions should be recommended and prescribed by a woman's health care provider in order to be absolutely sure they are safe for mom and baby. For example, diet pills, energy pills, and laxatives are rarely—if ever—needed to support a pregnancy. Think about it—laxatives may be used by some women to promote weight loss, but the only situations that warrant using laxatives while pregnant are those times when a woman is having

Teens can take complete ownership of their prenatal health and well-being by educating themselves on potential risk factors given their personal medical history and age, what activities they should avoid during pregnancy (like X-rays and tanning), and what to expect and plan for during each stage of their pregnancy through delivery.

trouble passing a bowel movement or having some other form of digestive distress and where she has her health care provider's blessing to take them. Teens should remember everything they eat or drink is passed on to baby, and their actions can directly impact their baby's development.

From smoking, drinking, and not eating healthy, to not having proper prenatal care, teens are much more likely than older women to have lifestyles that negatively impact the growth and development of their babies. This puts them at an increased risk for premature labor, low-birth-weight babies, and even miscarriages—not to mention the slew of risks that come with each of those issues for both baby and mom. However, teens have more control than they might think. The single, most impactful method of reducing teen-pregnancy-specific health and medical issues is for teens to find a health care professional they can trust and follow a prenatal care plan. They can choose to find a health care provider and follow his or her directives, or they can simply ignore the need to care for themselves and baby by not making their health and well-being a priority. Although some issues and complications can't be avoided, many can and teens alone wield a tremendous amount of control over the health and well-being of themselves and baby.

In Her Words: Q&A with Tara LaBerge

In 1983, five people sat around a table discussing the feasibility of offering a completely free Christian-based program to help low-income mothers and their families. Now, thirty-two years later, Mother and Unborn Baby Care (MUBC), located in Appleton, Wisconsin, provides material assistance, education, and emotional support to more than 150–200 clients and their children up to age three per year. Together with neighboring nonprofit WomanKind Medical Clinic, women can receive free pregnancy testing; limited ultrasounds; education on adoption, abortion, and parenting; medical referrals; and more. Although the program is Christian-based, it does support and help women of other faiths.

A key component to MUBC's success in fostering and growing its mission is its Earn While You Learn program for mothers. The educational program answers many of the questions pregnant mothers have about having a safe pregnancy, what to expect in childbirth, how to care for a newborn baby, mother and baby bonding, child care, self-esteem, shaken baby syndrome, sudden infant death syndrome, sexual integrity, discipline, life skills management, and raising kids with character. When moms complete an hour-long lesson, they earn Mommy Money they can use to purchase items such as maternity and baby clothes, blankets, diapers, formula, and, when available, cribs, strollers, and baby furniture—all of which are donated.

Tara LaBerge offers the organization's perspective and advice to help teens better navigate the world of parenting.

Author Jessica Akin (JA): Please share more about your organization's mission and its growth since inception.

Tara LaBerge (TL): Our mission is to support women with material things and support them emotionally. But, first and foremost, our mission is to save life.[e]

JA: What do teen parents struggle with the most?

TL: We see many teens struggle with a lack of financial resources to support themselves and their child/children. Also, it does take a certain level of maturity to know how to raise a child. Having children at such a young age can be difficult for teens. We see teens struggling with the patience it requires to handle day to day child rearing and the inevitable temper tantrums, not listening, and defiance that comes with babies and toddlers.

JA: What skills should they work on while they are pregnant to set them up for success as young parents?

TL: Learning about stages of development for the child's first year of life. Talking to other young and/or new moms about what to expect. Teens could also think about people they know who can help out when they need a break or who they can go to when they are struggling.

JA: What do you think should be primary concerns/priorities for teen parents as they start to raise their child/children?

TL: To be aware that they will need support, that they may become isolated as their friends are still in high school or college and in a different place in life than they are. Be aware that others may judge them. To be encouraged that just because they are young does not mean they can't be a good parent; it just might take a little more energy and determination, especially if still working on classes for graduation from high school.

JA: What differences do you see between the parenting style, engagement, and involvement between teen mothers and fathers? Does your organization support fathers as well as mothers in its educational outreach?

TL: Our organization does encourage teen fathers to come, but not many do. Therefore, we typically do not work with teen fathers.

JA: What is your advice for teen parents looking to finish high school and continue their educational goals?

TL: We encourage them to finish high school and even further their education, if at all possible, especially if they are living at home and have that support and help. Without even a basic high school diploma, it will be hard to get a job and support a child. Statistically, teen parents tend to live in poverty and/or have lower paying jobs because they tend to drop out and/or do not further their education.

JA: What other facts, messages, or information do you/your organization believe would be helpful for teen parents to hear and understand?

TL: To be aware of the importance and impact that choices they make can have on their child, starting from the time they are pregnant.

Want to learn more about MUBC or help support its mission? Reach out at fvmubc.org or by contacting it at 1-920-733-7334.

Try This! Start a Convo with Baby

You don't have to wait until the baby arrives to begin talking and communication with him or her. If it feels uncomfortable to just start talking to your growing belly, take the following advice from BabyCenter.com: "It's a great way to start the bonding process. If having an actual conversation seems odd to you, narrate your activities; read a book, magazine, or newspaper; or share your secret wishes for your child. This is great practice for after your baby's born. Talking to babies is one of the best ways to help them develop language skills."[f]

LIFE AFTER BABY

The reason this book doesn't feature any celebrity teen moms from popular shows is because MTV is not reality, and life after baby is a 24/7 rollercoaster of emotions, expectations, and responsibility. It may be entertaining to watch those young women and men, but at the end of the day, the lives of actual teen parents are anything but entertaining. It's hard—harder than they ever thought and wrought with sacrifices, struggles, and conflicting emotions.

Take, for example, teen mom Monica Meyer. Monica was sixteen when she found out she was pregnant. Prior to that, she had been very involved with her high school's student council. She had gone to leadership camps each summer and attended conferences throughout the year. She ran for an executive board position as a sophomore and was even elected! "I loved being involved and was very proud of my new role. I worked on countless committees planning dances, meeting up for hours making decorations and planning details of school events. I helped organize coat drives and supported other community programs," Monica said. She also played basketball and soccer her freshman and sophomore year. "I wasn't super good at basketball but had been playing with the same group of girls for years and loved being a part of that team. Because of my history of playing basketball and because of my height, I was recruited as a soccer goalie when they became in need of one. I tried out with the team and was excited to be needed and to try something new. I loved being a goalie."[1]

Try This! Name That Baby

● Have some fun with your partner or family members and think about possible baby names. BabyCenter.com suggests, "Make a list of ten names you like. Have your partner do the same. Trade lists and cross out one name on the other's list that you dislike. Keep taking turns until you have a set of names you can both live with. Talk about why you like and dislike certain names. Many couples even create ground rules, such as no names of former girlfriends or boyfriends and no names that have ever been used for family pets."[a]

Monica was living a life she loved and one filled with the fun and enjoyment of a typical teenager. She was even fiscally responsible as a teen. "To make money I babysat a ton growing up. I believe I was watching the neighbor kids occasionally by age eleven. It was a great job and for years I watched kids of families all over town, probably every weekend. At fifteen, I was working at a local pizza place. It was not managed well and we teenagers pretty much ran it. At sixteen I was working a lot of hours there. I worked with a good friend of mine and made other friends there and we had lots of fun," she said. But the fun soon turned into trouble. "My best friend and I had started smoking pot with some of the older kids working there. We hung out with them outside of work and dated a couple of the guys as well."[2]

Monica found out she was pregnant at sixteen. After taking several tests with a friend, she went to Planned Parenthood and the results were confirmed. "I told my mom that same night. I was pregnant for almost all of my junior year of high school. I was seventeen the summer I gave birth to my son."[3]

Life was never the same for Monica, and she shared her story in hopes that other pregnant teens will find the inspiration they need to find strength and get through this tough stage of their lives.

> My advice is to take it one day at a time. Life can absolutely be overwhelming. Things happen that may seem or are possibly even out of your control. You can only worry about yourself and not the actions of others. Be strong, allow help, and use the resources that are available. There are people and organizations out there that are willing to help guide you through a healthy pregnancy. Having a baby as a teenager is far from easy. It makes life difficult and often changes what may have been your plan for your future. In my experience, considering adoption as an option allowed possibilities for myself and my son. It ended up not being right for me, but I would highly recommend to anyone that isn't sure if they are ready to be a parent, to consider adoption. Overall, THIS TOO SHALL PASS. Time doesn't always heal, but it does change things . . . and if you do everything in your power to make the best of a situation, you will be able to look back and know you did everything you could.[4]

Monica's struggles and story aren't unique. In his article "Life as a Teen Father-to-Be," Thomas C. wrote about the reality of being a teen father and it's not glamourous. Real-life teen parents aren't receiving checks from production companies or getting media attention that can lead to additional income and resources. Real-life teen parents struggle to make ends meet and finish high school, deal with emotions they aren't necessarily prepared to deal with, and raise a child

In Her Words: Q&A with Teen Mom Monica

Monica shared her experience in hopes of helping teens realize that the life they've always dreamed of isn't out of reach—even if they have a baby. In the following Q&A, read more about her struggles not knowing whether to move forward with an adoption, dealing with the biological father not in the picture, going back to school to achieve her dream of becoming a nurse, and how having a baby changed every aspect of her life—for the better.

Author Jessica Akin (JA): What was your pregnancy experience like?

Monica Meyer (MM): My mom was exceptionally supportive my entire pregnancy. She drove me to all of my appointments. We talked to counselors and social service people to determine what my options were for keeping and raising a baby at seventeen or giving him up for adoption. There were a lot of great resources out there. I was well supported and had options laid out in front of me. I was able to read through biographies of families that were looking to adopt. Couples that wanted nothing more than to have a baby, that had gone through years of struggles to build a family, as I sat there at seventeen, unexpectedly pregnant and not knowing what to do. I was drawn to the story of one couple. They came from large families. The guy worked for Disney. I remember thinking they might be a great family to love my baby. I remember calling my contact at Lutheran Social Services and telling her that I had made up my mind. This couple would be a good fit for my baby and give him a better life than I felt like I could. I will never forget the woman's voice on the other end of the phone. She said that this particular couple had just found out that they were pregnant and not eligible in this program to adopt. I was upset and happy all at once. To this day I took it as my sign that I was supposed to keep my baby.

I wasn't completely sure though and was distraught in the decision making process on a daily basis. I had plans to finish school and go off to college with my friends. Raising a baby at seventeen was not in the big plan. I had three teenage brothers at the time. How could my mom support all of us and a new baby? How in the world could we make it all work???

One of my counselors gave me the option of having the baby go into foster care when we left the hospital to allow myself time to figure it all out. She said that it could help to not be pregnant while trying to make a life-changing decision. I could take a couple weeks if I needed, to decide what was best for my baby and me. That is what I ended up doing. I gave birth to a beautiful perfect baby boy. I held him in the rocking chair of the nursery at the hospital and cried and cried. This was indeed my baby but I needed to give him the chance at the best life possible. I would give myself some time after having him to decide if that life was with me or another family. It is still a blur to think I left the hospital without him. But I did. I needed to be sure. I spent the next couple weeks before my senior year of high school trying to figure it out. It became more and more apparent that there was no way I could live without him. He was my baby . . . and my family and I would raise him!

That was almost nineteen years ago.[b]

JA: How has life been after the baby? How has your life changed?

MM: Life after having a baby was a whirlwind in every way possible. When you think life can't possibly hand you anymore, it just might. My brother's best friend was killed a week after I brought my son home. He was like a brother to my brothers and I and another son to my mom. It was beyond devastating to all of us. My baby boy became a source of light and life for my entire family. He was the reason to get up each day and to know that brighter days lied ahead.

I had switched my school schedule to accommodate taking him to day care and working full time. I only needed two and a half credits to graduate my senior year so I went to school half days and then went to work. I had always been a good student and maintained that after having the baby. It was a proud day when I called my mom at work to tell her I had gotten my gold tassels the week of graduation, and that I would indeed be graduating with honors! Looking back at pictures from my graduation, in my cap and gown, holding my ten-month-old son, still makes me cry.

I was lucky. I had a wonderful family that were all a huge support system. I was able to finish school, go on to college, work a couple different jobs, and live at home with my son, all with the support of my family. They all took turns picking him up from the wonderful family across the street from us, that did day care out of their house, and they ended up being a huge part of my son's life. They took him on basically as one of their own. To this day I cannot thank them enough for that!

Because of all the help and support I had, I was able to live as some other teenagers did. I was still able to spend some time with friends, go to some school activities and games, and Homecoming and Prom. I worked a lot. I had more responsibilities than any of my friends. A few of them stuck around and wanted to be part of mine and Austin's life. To this day, those that were around, still are and have watched him grow up with me![c]

JA: How did the father take the news? What is his level of involvement today?

MM: My son's biological father was shocked when I told him. He had recently turned sixteen. We weren't necessarily "together." We dated and had mutual friends. While I was pregnant as a junior in high school, he was only a sophomore. I can only imagine all the comments and ridicule he received. He wasn't supportive. We weren't together. He had nothing to say. His mom ended up packing up and moving to Florida with him before the end of the pregnancy. He didn't come back or meet Austin until he was a year old. When he moved back, his intention was to finish high school and be a part of Austin's life. He never was able to keep it all together enough to do that. He lived with friends. They partied and that always seemed to be more important. I wasn't innocent in experimenting and partying myself, but I was the one that held down a couple jobs and went to night school, while he wanted the world to feel sorry for him. He would come to my mom's house occasionally to watch Austin when we were all off at school or work, but that was short lived. Having him in my mom's house was not a good idea. He stopped seeing him around age three. When I got married when Austin was five, he signed over his rights. He had never paid any kind of child support or was of any financial help. My husband legally adopted Austin when we got married. He is the only father Austin knows.

I always wanted to be honest with Austin about how things had gone and how they played out the way they did, but I found out when he became a teenager that perhaps I hadn't handled it the best. He felt uninformed when his friends realized how young I was when I had him, and that his "dad" wasn't his biological father. He didn't know how to respond to them, didn't feel comfortable or have all the answers he needed. I felt horrible at how sad he was. I always wanted him to be informed, but as he was growing up, I stuck to the concept of not giving him more information than he needed at certain ages. When I had brought it up over the years, he was never really interested, or possibly understood, since all he really remembered was the dad in his life every day.

I would imagine that Austin and his biological father will meet at some point, if and when Austin is interested or ready. Until then, thanks to all the amazing men in Austin's life, he has definitely not lacked in male role models!

JA: How did you finish school and manage to pursue your educational goals?

MM: School has been a continual process. I took night classes toward a business degree for a couple years while working full time during the day. After getting married and having two more beautiful boys, I didn't start taking classes again until my youngest was in preschool. At that point I knew I didn't want to be stuck in an office forever, so I transferred what credits I could and started taking prerequisite classes for a nursing program. I've done that part time as well, and after completing the LPN program, I took and passed my boards. I now work as an LPN within Children's Hospital. I plan to go back to finish my RN.

while they are still so young themselves. Thomas C. experienced the weight of the responsibility immediately. "When my girlfriend told me she might be pregnant, it made me feel like a father already, like I already had a big responsibility. I didn't feel ready for that responsibility, so I told her I thought she should get an abortion and she said, 'OK.' But next thing you knew, she already had a big belly."[5]

Pregnant teens and teen dads often struggle with wanting to protect their "normal" life during the pregnancy and struggle with their diminished freedom and feeling restricted after baby comes. Adulthood and motherhood come at a significant cost, and even when teens are living with parents or caregivers, they are going to experience feelings of being an adult and caring for their child, while still feeling as if they are being treated like a child by their parents.

Being a teen father isn't funny or entertaining and no person wants to have to tell another to get an abortion. The reality is lonely, scary, and overwhelming.

> ## Try This! Do Some Laundry
>
> ● Take all those cute sock sets, onesies, outfits, and blankets and toss them in the washing machine with gentle or sensitive hypoallergenic detergent to get all baby's clothing ready for him or her to wear upon his or her debut to the world.

Thomas C. writes, "I suddenly feel very old, as if I cannot do the things I used to like doing, like hanging out or sleeping over at my friends' houses. . . . Imagine, now I have to go and get a better job and support not only myself, but my son and my girlfriend." Thomas C. wants to be there for his child and is committed to working through his feelings and doing what it takes to be there emotionally and financially—but that's still a huge hurdle for him to overcome. "I want to try to provide my child with everything I can, including love. . . . But I know it's going to be hard. Being a 15 year old with no kids gives you the freedom to do all the things that teens want to do, like going to the movies, hanging out with your friends, going shopping for yourself, and spending all your money on video games. If you're a teenager who's going to be a father, get ready for no freedom for yourself or for the girl who's having the baby."[6]

In a post titled "I'm a Teen Father," littleboyblue16 wrote about his experience raising his first daughter, and subsequent children, and the trials he faced as a young thirteen-year-old father with little support from his or his partner's parents:

> I was almost 14 when my daughter Alexis (Lexy) was born. I took care of her full time from the time she was 1—now and I always will my 2nd and 3rd baby was born May 30th. I'm with their mom we raise them together even though I have to teach her stuff since they are her first babys [*sic*] and her parents say we had fun so now we are in charge with no help unless I have to be hospitalized like I do have to be many times. Most people yell at us and put us down but the way we see it is yes it's harder for us to work and be full time parents but not impossible. We take turns working so we don't have to rely on welfare nothing against it but I was raised on it and I want better for my kids.[7]

Then there's teen dad David. David shared his story through Washingteen Help, a program developed by WithinReach. WithinReach is a nonprofit organization that connects families and individuals to health and food resources. He speaks about not only his experience and the difficulties he encountered, but also

> ### Try This! Get Educated
>
> ● Labor, delivery, and then caring for a newborn are hard work. That's why many hospitals and medical facilities offer classes for new parents and parents-to-be. BabyCenter.com suggests doing research early and getting enrolled as soon as possible. "The best and most popular ones fill up fast so start your search now. Classes vary quite a bit in their approach. Some are spread out over several weeks, while others are as short as a day. Your hospital probably offers classes, but you may want to take a specialized class elsewhere. To find a class, call the International Childbirth Education Association at (952) 854–8660 for information about childbirth educators in your area."[d]

the need for teens to seek out and accept help. He was eighteen when his son was born and realized quickly after he found out that his girlfriend was pregnant that he was going to have to make some significant life changes in order to support both his roles as father and son. "I was happy and sad because I saw my future pass by me like crazy. I knew I had to make some changes as I grew up to become an adult and a teen dad. I had to learn real fast what it meant to be there for my family as a father, and a son to my parents." David made the choice to support his girlfriend through her entire pregnancy and feels this contributes to his connection and relationship with his son. "I can still remember our son stretch for more space . . . seeing his feet, letting him punch me in my hand. It felt like I spent quality time with my son even though he wasn't in my arms yet." He admits that he couldn't go at being a teen father alone and that teens who find themselves in a similar situation should develop a network of people to rely on, help them, and give them the additional support they need since they are not adults themselves. "From a father's point of view, I would have to say childbirth was exciting and scary. But knowing you have a support system with you it makes it feel much better."[8]

As these teen parents realize either during the pregnancy or after, many "typical" teen activities can either have a negative impact on themselves and the baby, or they just don't have the time anymore to participate in activities they used to love and find enjoyable. Their lives become centered on baby, trying to get through each day as parents, and better themselves by finishing school. While they can feel overwhelmed, scared, and anxious about their abilities as parents, teen parents can succeed.

Teens may still be up all night, but the party now features an infant! Teens may find them-selves less interested in aspects of their pre-baby lives as they adjust to and balance the demands of raising a child.

In Her Words: Q&A with Mom and Teen Advocate Barbara Bell

Barbara Bell is the Teen Tot Coordinator for the Milwaukee Adolescent Health Program at the Medical College of Wisconsin. Barbara has worked with teens for more than twenty-seven years and has been with the program since inception twenty-three years ago. The Teen Tot Program began with fourteen moms and babies and today supports more than forty moms and babies each year.

Barbara is passionate about the program and the need for consolidated health care for teen parents,

The program is designed so moms and babies see the same doctors. This means the child and mother stay up to date with check-ups, well baby visits, and immunizations. We support our teen mothers with comprehen-sive and reproductive healthcare. Our comprehensive healthcare includes health checks, immunizations, acute care visits for both mother/child. Our Reproductive Healthcare includes STD evaluations/treatment, and birth control management like Depo provera injections, Nexplanon insertions, Nuva rings, and oral contraception. Our goal is that mom and baby can come to one place for all their needs in sort of a one stop shop. We've found that if a mom has to go to multiple locations, they are less likely to be compliant with medical care for themselves as well as their child."[e]

Barbara's passion stems from her own young pregnancy and her belief that providing support to these young moms is part of her giving back.

It's a ministry to me. At age nineteen I had a baby. I'd been on my own since I was seventeen. It was just a neighbor that I'd befriended. I said no, he said yes, I said no, he said yes. I didn't know much about abortion, so I kept the baby. I was in the welfare system for two years and I met my husband when I was carrying my child, but I was so afraid of men and we developed a deep friendship before dating. So this is my passion to do what I do. Although my life is not like what some of these kids go through, there are some similarities. I want to be an advocate for these kids.[f]

Barbara sat down with me to talk about her experience and share her perspectives on how teen parents can succeed.

Author Jessica Akin (JA): Let's start before a teen gets pregnant. What could teens and their parents do better to prevent pregnancy?

Barbara Bell (BB): I feel that education is the most effective way to enlighten anyone in situations as sensitive as pregnancy prevention. We need to make sure that the parent or parents are comfortable and equipped with the proper information to help ensure that they are enforcing the right information to get a positive result from their children.

I think we have to learn to listen to what's happening instead of pointing a finger. We live in a society that says everything is okay. Maybe the teen was lonely, or was coerced, or society said it was okay. So they had sex. There are so many instances and we have to treat people as people, not as metaphors. Then we can start to help.

We need more parent involvement from the teen's parents. I say this because we may have kids who may be thinking about or they are already sexually active and not on birth control, but feel they can't talk with a parent because of the sensitivity of this topic. This individual will do one or two things: (1) talk with a friend who may be the same age as the one with questions regarding this issue, or (2) they heard about where they can go to get some help to prevent an unwanted pregnancy. Some may start off on birth control without the consent of a parent and become noncompliant because of the follow-up that is required by the medical doctor and will taper off because they are too afraid to discuss this matter with a parent. Some parents have a perception that if we put teens on birth control, they will have sex. Some kids are trying to be responsible and protect themselves, but their parents need to be educated to understand what we're dealing with. Peer pressure comes in many forms, and sexuality is another form of peer pressure.

We have parents that are too busy. We had a fifteen-year-old who delivered her own baby. The parents didn't realize they had a pregnant teen living in their home. Mom worked third and first shifts, dad worked first and second shifts. The teen went into the bathroom, labored, delivered, cut the umbilical cord, cleaned the baby, and went to bed. Dad felt like he had to go back home and when he was heading up the stairs, he heard the infant crying. There was the baby on the towel lying in the bed with his daughter who just delivered her own baby. I said to her, you told your parents that you didn't know you were pregnant but how'd you know what to do when you did what you did to deliver the baby? She said she looked it up on the Internet. She had a healthy baby, but can you imagine what could have gone wrong?

Even though we teach our children good values, send them to school public or private, and they may be in a good group; there is social media, TV, radio, and music that's suggestive and the thoughts start to occur. We have to educate the parents, or get educated as parents, so we can develop a relationship with our sons and daughters, so we can communicate with our children. Be their parent not their friend. A parent wears many hats and sometimes we as parents may not have the answer to every situation, but we all learn from trial and error. In other words don't give up. Know and understand that our children are gifts from God.

You can't expect someone to do what he or she has never been taught.[9]

JA: What do you see as the biggest hurdles teen parents face?

BB: No one knows until you find yourself in this situation that you should have or could have waited to become a parent at a young age. Taking care of a baby is a huge responsibility whether rich or poor. Our foster care system is bursting at the seams because of children born too soon by way of teen parents. It has become a vicious cycle, and this vicious cycle leaves nothing short of broken lives and dreams right here in America. This is not an urban issue; it is a people issue. There are not enough systems set in place to help eradicate this problem. There should be schools (high schools and middle schools) that house day care and job training facilities to help young teen fathers know what it means to work and support his family. There are single parents that are raising their own children on a low or fixed income that can't achieve their own dreams because of an unexpected teen pregnancy within their home, and there is nothing set in place to assist this family. There are a lot of unique situations within our society.

I have one teen mother who came to us for her baby's two-week checkup. After routine questioning and examination before starting this mother on birth control she said she wasn't sexually active, but three months later when she came in for follow-up and birth control, she was pregnant. Now she is the mother of two kids at sixteen. She got on birth control, again. Her mother (the teen's mom) was a single mom with three other children. Now, they have her four children and two grandbabies. You can't expect anyone to do something they don't know. Now the vicious cycle has begun in another family that could have used parent intervention.

JA: What do you feel should be top of mind or primary concerns/priorities for teen parents?

BB: There should be mandatory parenting classes so the teen can properly assist the needs of their child. Again, the school should have programs implemented that provide day care and short school days, tutors to help teen parents to graduate school. Later clinic hours so that a teen parent can be compliant with medical care for herself as well as her child.

JA: What differences do you see between the parenting style, engagement, and involvement between teen moms and dads?

BB: Women by nature are a lot more nurturing then the male species for some reason. There appears to be more opportunity for young women than men. When a young girl gets pregnant and delivers, we counsel more females about abstinence and birth control than males.

JA: What are the biggest health risks for teen moms during pregnancy? Is there anything teens should be aware of that is unique to their age demographic while pregnant?

BB: Let me say this: teens have been having babies at a young age for centuries. Our bodies are wonderfully made; a woman was created to bear children. Anyone is at risk for the unexpected once we conceive a child. We consider teens at risk because of the possible infections, multiple partners, little or no prenatal care, low self-esteem, or mental anguish. Prenatal care is vital for both the mother and the unborn child.

JA: Can you share some stories or anecdotes from your experiences with teens telling their parents/caregivers they are pregnant? What have you seen as successful methods for sharing?

BB: Our clinic visits are designed to create a relationship between patient and provider so that the patient feels comfortable to share with us any concerns that they may have—even having a desire to start on birth control without the consent of a parent. Our visits may start out with the parent in the exam room and eventually the parent is asked to step out. Not to disrespect the parent, but we have learned down through the years that the teen will open up about some issues that they do not feel comfortable talking about with the parent in the room. With that being said, we then are capable to provide the care that is needed, and there have been times the unexpected has happened where both parties are surprised. There are a lot of emotions (fear, hurt, pain, sadness, regrets, uncertainty, and doubt). What we do is reschedule the patient for a week's time to come back to discuss their final decision (deliver, abort, or place child up for adoption). We find that if you give the situation enough space that person will most likely make a decision that he or she is willing to live with.

JA: Can you share any stories about successful teen parents? How did they structure their days or lives to support themselves and their child/children?

BB: Our teen mother who had gotten pregnant for the second time at fifteen years old and is a mother of three at age twenty-one graduated from high school at age nineteen and is pursuing a college degree in nursing at a community college. I am so Godly proud of her. No, it was not easy going to school during the day and attend to children's needs, homework, going without missing a day; and living at home with her mother, three other siblings and her own children, but perseverance prevailed.

JA: What has been your experience with helping teens deal with facing judgments or criticism?

BB: No one is perfect and we all make mistakes, but we all can learn from our mistake by not allowing ourselves to become vulnerable to the same situation again. I always tell them that there is greatness in all of us, and we will never reach our full potential if we never try. One day at a time, if you work with life, life will work with you. Bad times don't last forever. You are in the driver's seat of your life; it's up to you which direction you will go in.

JA: What other facts or information do you believe would be helpful for teen parents to hear and understand?

BB: I sometimes think within myself, "I wish people would just tell the truth." What do I mean? That being a teen parent is not what it's all cracked up to be; babies are adorable but they are also hard work and I never have time for myself, nor do I get to enjoy some of the things other people my age enjoy.

JA: What message would you like to personally share with teen parents?

BB: That being a strong parent is achievable. It's just hard. You have to be willing to put in the time. Because it's going to take time. If you have a black scuffmark on the floor, you can't just wipe it. You need the right chemicals and you need to scrub.

JA: What is your ultimate dream to helping teen parents?

BB: A lot of things are in place, but not designed to help. There needs to be flexibility to provide the care teens need. It's not about what's written down; policy makers and officials need to get into the trenches and understand the problems teens and medical professionals are facing. There are so many entities willing to help too and if we would really work together, the school, the home, the church, the grocery store, etc., we could collectively make a difference.

I would love to see a campus with a doctor's office, school, and day care to create a cocoon so that while teen parents are in it, they can learn in a safe and supported environment. Then, when they're ready, they can fly into society.

I want to share the truth. If we are looking at it from a medical standpoint, teen pregnancy can be black and white. But, there's nothing in the medical books to help them with this. This isn't just the urban life. It's a universal problem, which is sad. It's not specifically one demographic. The kids are hurting and depressed, because no one is listening to them. There is so much going in this society that people, and young people, are dealing with. Even though I've been doing this for years, it's real.

The kids are screaming for help and we can't just walk out of here.

Ten Keys to Success

Parenting is not easy and being a teen parent presents a multitude of challenges to overcome. But teens can do it. They can provide a good life for themselves and their child with hard work and determination, and by believing in themselves and their abilities when times get tough. Although some of the suggestions may seem repetitive because they've been discussed throughout this book, here are the top ten things teens can do to help themselves succeed.

Learn More!
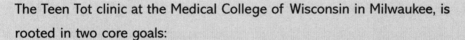

The Teen Tot clinic at the Medical College of Wisconsin in Milwaukee, is rooted in two core goals:

1. To provide convenient, comprehensive, health care to teenage mothers and their children
2. To foster a more positive future for the mother and child by preventing repeat teen pregnancy and promoting high school graduation

The Teen Tot clinic offers a health education program to teach and reinforce positive parenting skills, infant nutrition, normal infant development of cognitive and motor skills, and academic achievement and promotion of high school attendance and graduation.

For more information about this program, visit www.mcw.edu/mahp.htm. Teens can e-mail health questions to teendoc@mcw.edu and trust that their questions and any answers received are confidential.

1. Find Quality Child Care

Many parents consider finding child care their single most important task before the baby comes. Even women who consider themselves stay-at-home moms usually have a network of sitters and child care options secured in case they need additional support, want to meet a friend sans kids, have errands to run, or need to make a doctor's appointment. Having someone you can rely on and trust to take care of your child cannot be understated. Many teens cite lack of child care, having to stay home with baby, and not having enough support to help with baby as the primary reasons for not finishing high school or pursuing their postsecondary educational and career goals. If cost is prohibiting you from finding child care, don't get discouraged; get creative. Have friends or even acquaintances in a similar situation? Offer to watch their little one on days that work for you and see if they can watch your little one when you need it. You can also do some research and a bit of paperwork to apply for federal or state programs that reimburse or provide funds for child care. Many local church or religious institutions often of-fer scholarships for those in need and organizations like the YMCA provide very cost-effective child care programs that are reputable, safe, and fun. Don't have access to a computer or phone to make the calls and do the research you need to? Go to your local library where resources are plentiful and available.

2. Finish High School

Let's be honest here—a traditional high school setting may not be the most con-ducive for teen parents, especially mothers, to finish and receive their diplomas. Teens may feel like outcasts and struggle with the comments and glares sent in their direction. Even if a teen doesn't experience any ridicule, morning sickness could prevent her from making some classes and the birth and delivery of her child may also take her away from studies for an extended time period. While traditional high school programs may not be able to tailor curriculum to support a teen pregnancy, this reality doesn't necessarily have to mean teens settle for being dropouts. There are many, many nontraditional and accredited programs. Several institutions offer online courses through which students can earn their diploma or GED. If you think these programs are less than or substandard—think again. Stanford University and Brigham Young University both offer online high school diploma programs that are considered highly elite and hard to get into.

That being said, you do have to do adequate research to make sure the online program you choose is reputable. Look for programs that allow you to transfer your existing credits, are accredited through the U.S. Department of Education and other national and regional accrediting agencies, and are state approved. If a school isn't up front about its accreditations and won't let you transfer your cur-rent credits, keep looking. Also, you want to be sure the institution you receive your diploma from is approved in that specific state. This should be clearly com-municated by the institution, and, again, if it's not, then keep looking. There are state-specific and national programs available with a range of fees, structures, and requirements to best fit individual students. Public and charter online schools are government-funded programs and typically are free to resident minors. While free sounds good, do your research early and complete the required paperwork well in advance. Every state's department of education lists funded online pro-grams so you can check these out at any time. Be prepared too for a little less flex-ibility. Online public schools have strict guidelines and limited course selections, and often cater only to certain geographical areas and districts. More costly op-tions include private and college-sponsored online high school diploma programs. These come at a cost, which can range up to and surpass $10,000 per year, but offer extensive course options, virtually unlimited flexibility, and the potential to transfer courses for college credits. Ultimately, the decision is yours to make, but the statistics couldn't be more clear . . . those teens who finish their high school education are more successful throughout the course of their lives.

3. Determine Your Passions and Career Goals

If you received a million dollars today and could do anything, what would you do? Obviously, this is never going to happen, but the question remains . . . if you had the resources and support to do anything with your life, what would it be? Give this some serious thought. As you've read throughout this book, continuing your education past high school will not only financially benefit you, but it could also make you a happier person and better parent. Make sure you take the time to figure out what you're passionate about. Investing in your future will require money, often requires you to sacrifice time with your child, and can put your social life on hold for a period of time, so it helps to be sure you're committed and excited about your future plans. You can start by thinking about what you're good at, or what others think you're good at, and then explore careers that capitalize on those traits.

Check out filmmaker and director Tiffany Shlain's film *The Science of Character*, which explores the neuroscience and social science that proves that we can shape who we are and who we want to be.[9] Or read and take the extensive quizzes in Gallup executive Tom Rath's *StrengthFinder 2.0* book, which highlights thirty-four traits and offers insight into how each can be successful and developed into jobs and careers.[10] You can even sit down and talk with your high school guidance counselor to see if there are tests or quizzes that can give you a better idea about your natural aptitudes. Take that insight into your local college and, for

---

▌ Try This! Pack Your Bag

● Around the time you're eight to eight and a half months pregnant, you'll want to start putting together your hospital bag. *Mommy Mentionables* blog suggests packing the following items to make mom and baby more comfortable during their stay: socks with grips, slippers, toiletries like toothpaste and favorite cosmetics, change for any vending machines or the cafeteria, swaddling blankets, phone charger, extra pillows or a favorite pillow, and finally a going home outfit for mom and baby. HospitalBag.org offers a free printable checklist of what to include in your hospital bag at http://www.hospitalbag.org/print-hospital-bag-checklist.PDF.

free, talk with an admissions counselor or career coach about the various jobs he or she has seen in those areas. Or, hit the Internet and do a web search for jobs you think you'd love. Let's say you always wanted to be a writer. Doing a web search will show you the huge diversity of jobs available for a writer. You will find jobs that aren't just related to authors and poets: technical writers write manuals and policies, marketing writers create brochures and copy for ads, and editors review books. There are grant and proposal writers, journalists, code writers and programmers, freelance writers, ghost writers . . . the list goes on. Doing some research allows you to explore and maybe even stumble upon a job and career you didn't even know existed!

4. Teen Fathers: Get In and Stay Involved

There is no getting around it: a father's involvement in his children's lives has a direct impact on a child's academic performance, behavior, sexual activity, potential for teen pregnancy, substance abuse, and incarceration. The more involved a father, the more positive the impact. Show up. Be present. Don't walk away—ever. As Mark/WiseTeenDad says, teen fathers can bond with their child (or children) in so many ways that don't involve a lot of money or resources: "Feed them, play with them, sing to them, read them books, change those diapers! It starts with having a good relationship with momma. If you've got at least a decent relationship there, you'll have a much easier time creating a strong connection with your baby. As your baby grows it becomes even more important to talk with them every day and ensure they know just how much you love them. Human beings need to feel loved, and especially need to feel that love from their father and mother. There's nothing stronger than the parent child bond."[11]

5. Develop a Support System

The African proverb "It takes a village to raise a child" is so often quoted because it's true. No one can be everything to his or her child, watch his or her child every second of every day, or provide everything for his or her child. Today's world is incredibly complex, fast paced, and wrought with challenges and opportunities. Children need strong parents, but they also need to see that they can rely upon others. As humans, we connect with and rely on each other in almost every aspect of our day. If you don't have one already, it's imperative that you create a community around yourself of people who inspire, motivate, encourage, and support you as an individual and teen parent. Join groups and organizations, get involved at your local church or religious institution, connect with other teen parents, and work on any strained relationships that you value.

The more teen fathers are involved in the lives of their children, the better off the children will be. Fathers can be engaged and present by playing with their kids, teaching and reading to them, and helping out the mother of their child or children, whether by picking up around the house or through financial support.

6. Put Together a Family Plan

Another important key to your success is preventing any further unintended pregnancies. Commit to not having another untimed, unwanted, and unplanned pregnancy again by coming up with a family plan and goals that include knowing how big a family you desire and how far apart you want your children. Your family plan should be entirely based on your values, life goals, and the resources you have available. Once you are aware of and excited about your family goals, the next step is preventing another pregnancy until you are ready. Talk with your health care provider about your plan and inquire about the various contraceptives and birth control solutions available that best meet your needs and goals.

7. Educate Yourself on Child Development

You'll be far better equipped to support and nurture your children as they age if you know where they should be from a developmental perspective and understand what milestones are appropriate at each age. Check out books like these: *The Wonder Years: Helping Your Baby and Young Child Successfully Negotiate the Major Developmental Milestones* (2007) by the American Academy of Pediatrics and Tanya Remer Altmann; *Your Child's Growing Mind: A Guide to Learning and Brain Development from Birth to Adolescence* (1994) by Jane Healy; *Caring for Your Baby and Young Child: Birth to Age 5* (fifth edition, 2009) by the American Academy of Pediatrics; and *Touchpoints, Birth to 3* (2006) and *Touchpoints, 3 to 6* (2002) by T. Berry Brazelton and Joshua D. Sparrow. These books offer insight into the many developmental milestones parents should be aware of as well as ways to bond, better understand, and connect with your child.

8. Never Stop Learning

Parenting is a never-ending job and it doesn't come with a user manual. There are so many different approaches, theories, and opinions on virtually every aspect of parenting, which can be overwhelming for new and younger parents. But the diversity and volume of topics are great news! There's rarely a right or wrong answer, and you are allowed and encouraged to pick and choose what works best for you as a parent. Ask questions and read everything you can about parenting. If you're not sure how to get a baby to latch on, go online and see what experts say or call your doctor. Curious how often you should feed or change baby's diaper? Ask your health care provider, ask an experienced mom, or do a search online. Issues like getting baby to sleep through the night and potty training are things every parent deals with. There's a plethora of websites, books, and articles discussing and dissecting every aspect of sleep patterns, sleep schedules, potty training incentives, and more that you can learn from. The point is to never give up—never think you have all the answers and never think you don't know what you're doing; no parent knows! You're not alone and the best thing you can do is reach out to other parents, your health care provider, books, and the Internet to educate yourself.

9. Consciously Co-parent

Not in a relationship with your partner? Then you'll really benefit from understanding what it means to co-parent and develop appropriate emotional boundaries

> ### ❚ Try This! Bath Time
>
> • Bath time can be a super fun experience, but for new parents, it can also be super scary. Some basic rules are to never leave your child alone in the bath tub, keep water temperature below 120 degrees, make sure all sharp objects like razors and scissors are out of your child's reach, keep the area around the tub dry, and empty the tub as soon as bath time is over.[h]

in order to create a relationship that's focused solely on the health and well-being of your shared child. Whether it's over coffee, text, e-mail, or phone, make a point to regularly communicate about your child and do you best to keep any judgments, emotions, and feelings out of the conversations. Both parents should work to shift their attention from any personal issues to the needs of their child and their child's ability to thrive within two separate households. If you don't understand your rights or need more assistance in coming up with a co-parenting plan, many states offer free mediation services that provide a social worker to help couples navigate custody agreements and work together to jointly develop a plan covering all aspects of shared custody. Your state may even offer mandatory or optional co-parenting-specific courses for free or at a nominal fee and if that's not an option, there are several private organizations that offer online co-parenting classes.

10. Believe in Yourself

It will take more time, effort, and energy to succeed. Look for a solution to every roadblock, challenge, and obstacle instead of an excuse for why you can't move forward. Like any parent, you can do this. You can be rock-star mom or fabulous family-man dad. You can overcome every statistic, perception, and stereotype. You can shape your own future and that of your child in an incredibly positive light. Believe in yourself, educate yourself, and never give up.

ORGANIZATIONS AND PROGRAMS

Although many organizations and institutions were either profiled or mentioned throughout this book, this chapter includes a more exhaustive list of organizations and programs dedicated to helping teen parents. Included in each listing is a bit about what's offered and contact information. Teens can also check out a list of resources such as books and movies starting on page 201.

Although there are many programs and organizations included below, this list is by no means all-encompassing. Also, notably missing from the list are organizations specifically dedicated to preventing teen pregnancy, of which there are

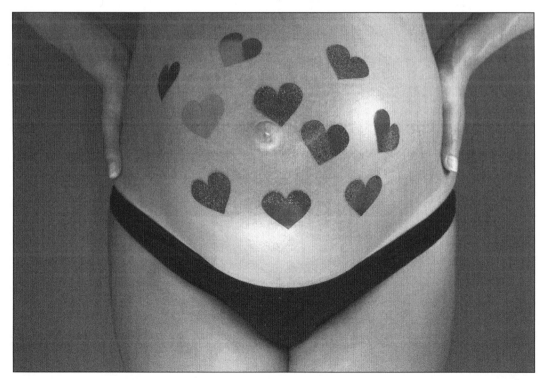

Teens should do what they can to ensure a healthy and happy pregnancy! There are a significant number of organizations and institutions eager to help teen moms and dads. With a little research, teens can uncover a wealth of support and create a deep network to rely upon when they need it most.

many. Here's why: clearly, being a teen parent isn't easy and efforts advocating making responsible decisions around sexual health are imperative. That being said, once teens become parents, they need access to information that helps them ensure a safe and healthy pregnancy and become strong parents.

Programs and Organizations

How to Use This List

Teen parents should use this list as a starting point and then complete more research in their own states, cities, towns, and communities. Pregnant teens can apply for a variety of federal and state-funded programs for financial help. Teens should start by researching what programs are made available by their state and local governments, which can include rent, child care, nutritional, and even tuition assistance. Adoption agencies and charitable services also provide financial assistance to teen parents, and reaching out to local agencies and charities in their communities could help connect teens to other teen parents and also open them up to more opportunities.

Teens should always remember that the health and well-being of themselves and their child before, during, and after pregnancy are their responsibility. While there are many people and places throughout the nation that are eager to help, it's up to teens as individuals to seek out support.

A Great Place to Start: Single Mother's Guide

The Single Mother's Guide is an incredible resource geared toward, you guessed it, single mothers. Even if you're not a single mom the site is still worth a visit as it does a great job of distilling and profiling many federal and state-sponsored and supported programs. You'll get the skinny on what each offers, high-level requirements, and even links to where to apply. Check out what programs are available in your state at www.singlemotherguide.com/state-assistance.

Adoption Connection

Adoption Connection works with pregnant women and their families (often called birth parents) anywhere in the United States. Visit www.adoptionconnection.org, call 1-800-972-9225, or text 415-355-4636 with questions for more information.

Bethany Christian Services

Bethany Christian Services is a global nonprofit organization that brings families together and keeps families together. Its services include adoption, foster care, and pregnancy counseling. It also provides counseling to families, assists refugees and immigrants resettling in the United States, and partners with several international countries to help keep families together. Visit www.bethany.org or call 1-800-238-4269 for more information.

Child Care Subsidy Program

Offered in all fifty states, the Child Care Subsidy Program helps offset child care costs by providing assistance to eligible families with children younger than thirteen. Each state has its own guidelines and application process so it's important to research your own state's requirements. The Single Mother's Guide actually profiles each state and includes a link on where to apply.

Covenant House

Founded in 1972, the Covenant House's mission is to help homeless kids escape the streets. It provides care and support to homeless, abandoned, abused, trafficked, and exploited youth through its network of twenty-seven "houses" throughout the United States, Canada, and Latin America. It also has a program dedicated to teen mothers and their children, which includes counseling, skill building, on-site child care, and more so that teen mothers can complete their education. Visit www.covenanthouse.org for more information. If you need counseling or shelter, please call 1-800-RUNAWAY or visit www.1800runaway.org twenty-four hours a day, seven days a week, 365 days a year.

March of Dimes

The organization is dedicated to helping moms have healthy babies. Research and information across all aspects of pregnancy are provided, as well as resources specifically for teen parents. It's also a great resource on pregnancy loss. Share Your Story is the March of Dimes' online community where families who have lost a baby can talk to and comfort each other, http://share.marchofdimes.org/. It offer frees brochures to help parents cope with their loss and the resulting grief.

Teens can order the following topics: *From Hurt to Healing*, *When You Want to Try Again*, and *What Can You Do* by visiting www.marchofdimes.org/loss/from-hurt-to-healing.aspx. Visit www.marchofdimes.org for its homepage.

Medicaid

The Affordable Care Act has made receiving affordable health insurance, including reproductive and prenatal care and well child visits and preventive services for your child, more accessible for the uninsured, low-income, and single parents living throughout the United States. Learn more about the program, eligibility, coverage, and options by visiting www.healthcare.gov or by calling 1-800-318-2596.

National Healthy Mothers, Healthy Babies

Its mission is to improve the health and safety of mothers, babies, and families through education and collaborative partnerships of public and private organizations. Its online library includes webinars, interviews with experts, and a lot of other great information about having a heathy pregnancy, labor and delivery, and parenting. Visit www.hmhb.org/about-us/our-programs.

Planned Parenthood

Planned Parenthood provides educational programs and outreach to 1.5 million young people and adults every year through its online community and fifty-nine unique, locally governed affiliates nationwide. With more than seven hundred health centers, Planned Parenthood gives teens access to information and resources, often for free, encompassing all aspects of sexual and reproductive health. Visit www.plannedparenthood.org or call 1-800-230-PLAN to learn more, find a health care center near you, and even book an appointment.

Section 8 Housing

Section 8 is a federally funded program that runs a network of more than 2,200 state and local housing agencies and provides vouchers to low-income families to help them afford decent and safe housing. Learn if you are eligible and what requirements you may need to meet by visiting the U.S. Department of Housing and Urban Development at www.hud.gov.

Standup Girl

Run by teen mom Becky, Standup Girl is a site offering encouragement, support, and a community for pregnant teens. The site includes information about pregnancy symptoms, fetal development, ultrasound images, and stories from girls who considered abortion as an option for unplanned pregnancy. Check it out at www.standupgirl.com.

Teens for Life

Teens for Life is an outreach of Indiana Right to Life, a not-for-profit organization working to restore and protect the sanctity of life and a state-level affiliate of the National Right to Life Committee. Pregnant teens or those who think they might be pregnant can call, text, e-mail, or IM a national CareNet hotline that offers free access to counselors who can help teens understand their options, deal with tough emotions, and receive compassionate support. Visit www.teensforlife.com/pregnant-we-can-help or call 1-800-395-HELP

Temporary Assistance for Needy Families (TANF)

The U.S. Office of Family Assistances offers the TANF program. The program helps needy families achieve self-sufficiency. TANF provides monthly cash stipends via Electronic Benefit Transfer, which is used like a bank debit card to pay for rent, day care, and even food. Check out the program by visiting www.acf.hhs.gov/programs/ofa/programs/tanf/about or calling 1-202-401-9275. Apply for assistance at your local or county welfare office. Not sure where that is? Locate your state contact information at www.acf.hhs.gov/programs/ofa/help or e-mail the Office of Family Assistance at www.acf.hhs.gov/programs/ofa/faq/how-do-i-apply-for-temporary-assistance-for-needy-families-tanf.

2houses

Can't get along with your child's mother or father? Take the personal aspect out of it completely with the online tool provided by 2houses. 2houses is an online interface and platform designed to help separated parents organize their child's schedule and keep track of all activities, manage any expenses, and easily exchange school, after-school, and medical information. While the software comes at a fee, 2houses also offers co-parenting e-books, guides, and information for free. Check it out here: www.2houses.com/en/tools.

Women, Infants and Children (WIC)

WIC is a supplemental nutrition program for pregnant women, breastfeeding women, women who had a baby within the last six months, infants, and children under the age of five. Visit www.adph.org/wic or call 1-888-WIC-HOPE to see if you meet income and nutritional risk requirements.

State-by-State Guide

The state guide below includes organizations specifically offering teen-related support and services. Don't see your state? Don't worry—this list is just a sampling to get you started on your research. You are encouraged to check out what's offered in your state and then do additional research on many more organizations in your local areas and communities that provide teen pregnancy support and services. See something you'd be interested in learning more about, but it's not in your state? Give the organization a call and ask if it knows of similar organizations in your area. It could have insight and access to resources that aren't posted or available online.

Alabama

Family Guidance Center of Alabama. Provides counseling, teen pregnancy, early childhood, family planning, and employment services and support. Visit familyguidancecenter.org or call 1-800-499-6597.

Alaska

CPC Pregnancy Center of Anchorage. Provides free services including pregnancy tests, STD tests, and information regarding pregnancy and abortion for women. Visit www.cpcanchorage.com or call the 24/7 Helpline at 877-791-5475.

Anchorage Health Center. Provides a Perinatal Program that provides support for women throughout their pregnancy experience, including obtaining eligibility for programs like Denali Kid Care, regular appointments during pregnancy, group pregnancy classes, in-hospital deliveries, postpartum depression screening, well child checkups, and support and referrals. Visitanhc.org or call 1-907-743-7200.

Arizona

Teen Outreach Pregnancy Services. Provides classes and courses, support groups, and on-site services. Information covering all aspects of teen pregnancy like making informed decisions about pregnancy, labor and delivery, parenting, teen father resources, and sexual health are included online. Visit www.teenoutreachaz.org or call 1-877-882-2881 for more information and locations.

Carenet Pregnancy Center of Cochise County. Provides a twenty-four-hour help line; pregnancy testing; education on pregnancy and fetal development; adoption referrals; STD/STI information; information about abortion procedures and alternatives; help dealing with parents, boyfriends, husbands, and other relationships; and referrals for medical care and social services like WIC (Women, Infants, and Children), AHCCCS (Arizona Health Care Cost Containment System), and DES (Department of Economic Security). PACE (Post-Abortion Counseling and Education), a support group for women, and Earn While You Learn programs for both moms and dads. Visit carenetpregnancy-sv.com/index.php or call 1-520-459-5683.

Reachout Pregnancy Center. Provides pregnancy testing, ultrasounds, counseling, and referrals for medical care and social services. Visit www.reachout womenscenter.com or call 1-520-321-4300.

California

Adolescent Family Life Program. Provides comprehensive case management services to pregnant and parenting teens and their children. Visit www.cdph.ca.gov/programs/aflp/Pages/default.aspx for program information and eligibility.

Cal-Learn Program, a statewide program for pregnant and parenting teens in the California Work Opportunity and Responsibility to Kids (CalWORKs) program. Provides services to help pregnant and parenting teens graduate from high school or its equivalent, become independent, and form healthy families. Visit www.cdss.ca.gov/cdssweb/PG84.htm for program information and eligibility.

Colorado

Florence Crittenton Services of Colorado, a Denver-based nonprofit. Provides educational resources to prepare and empower teen moms to be productive members of the community. Using a comprehensive and evidence-based approach, the agency offers a spectrum of wraparound services for the entire teen family, including academics, career guidance, and parenting training for pregnant and parenting teen mothers at the Florence Crittenton High School; early childhood education for their infants and toddlers at the Qualistar-rated Early Learning Center; and counseling, education, and parenting support for teen mothers and their family members through the Student and Family Support Services. Check it out at www.flocritco.org.

Connecticut

Center for Children's Advocacy. Provides educational resources and support to help children and teens succeed through projects and programs. Visit www .kidscounsel.org for details on its programs and more information.

Florida

Young Parents Program, a voluntary alternative placement program serving pregnant or parenting youth who are no older than twenty-two years of age. Provides students an opportunity to continue their education and to receive prenatal and parenting classes such as Health for Expectant Parents; Parenting I; Parenting II; Nutrition and Wellness; Personal Health II; and Personal, Social, and Family Relations. Other required academic courses are offered to Young Parent Program students through the Florida Virtual School, PLATO, and through direct instruction. Visit ctae.edu/about-ctae/other-services/young-parent-program or call 1-352-671-7200 for more information and locations.

Georgia

Georgia Agape. Provides faith-based unplanned pregnancy counseling assistance, professional Christian counseling, adoption and foster care support, and family life enrichment seminars and workshops. Visit www.georgiaagape.org or call 1-770-452-9995 for more information.

Illinois

Teen Parent Connection. Provides extensive programming and education for teen parents, including long-term assistance for self-esteem development, parenting skills, and empowerment toward self-sufficiency. Visit teenparentconnection.org or call 1-630-790-8433 for more information.

Indiana

Eskenazi Health Teen Care and Wellness. Provides teen-focused care, including help with menstrual issues and birth control methods, pregnancy testing, prenatal and infant care, and pediatric/well-baby care for infants and children. See more at www.eskenazihealth.edu/our-services/teen-care-and-wellness-program.

Iowa

United Action for Youth. Provides a Teen Parent Program featuring one-on-one support and education on creating a nurturing home environment, child development, positive discipline, role modeling, and age-appropriate expectations to have for children. Visit www.unitedactionforyouth.org/content/?page_id=129 or call 1-319-338-7518 for more information.

Kansas

Rachel House. Provides free pregnancy tests, free ultrasounds, and abortion education in the Kansas City area. Call 1-816-921-5050 or 1-800-712-HELP for more information or to schedule an appointment.

Kentucky

Avenues for Women. Provides state-licensed medical assistance to girls and women facing unplanned pregnancies. Visit avenuesforwomen.com or call 1-502-695-0500 for more information on services and locations.

Louisiana

Healthy Start New Orleans. Provides services to residents of Orleans Parish who are pregnant or parenting children under the age of two. Healthy Start promotes healthy communities by nurturing healthy pregnancies, healthy babies, and healthy families. Call 1-504-658-2600 to sign up for Healthy Start or find out more about the programs available.

Maine

The Maine Children's Home. Provides counseling services, international and domestic adoption support, early child care, and mentoring and practical life skill development for teen parents. Visit www.mainechildrenshome.org/index.php or call 1-207-873-4253 for more information.

Massachusetts

Massachusetts Alliance on Teen Pregnancy. Provides resources and respect-building programs for teen parents. Check out its programs and locations at www.massteen pregnancy.org/young-people/ma-expectant-and-parenting-teen-programs.

Minnesota

Annex Teen Clinic. Provides birth control and pregnancy testing, STI screenings, sex education, and teen pregnancy support services. Visit annexteenclinic.org or call 1-763-533-1316 for more information, locations, and to make an appointment.

Missouri

Mother's Refuge. Provides services to pregnant women, ages twenty-one or younger, and their babies who have no permanent place to live and who are continuing their education. Teens receive a loving home, clothing, food, access to medical care, education, infant and parenting classes, and practical life skills while living at Mother's Refuge. Visit www.mothersrefuge.org/index or call 1-816-353-8070 for more information and locations.

Barnes Jewish Hospital Teen Pregnancy Center. Provides pregnancy support, medical attention, and resources to pregnant adolescents who are seventeen years old or younger. In addition to the medical examination, educational and support services such as nutritional counseling, childbirth, and parenting and life skills classes are part of the prenatal visits. Visit www.barnesjewish.org/obstetrics-gynecology/teen-pregnancy for more information and locations.

Missouri Volunteer Resource Mothers. Provides emotional support and parenting techniques during and after pregnancy to pregnant/parenting young mothers and fathers. St. Louis Volunteer Resource Parents and St. Louis County Volunteer Resource Parents matches pregnant/parenting teens with trained volunteer mentors. Visit www.frcmo.org/services/helping-teens/teenparentmentoring to find out more about eligibility requirements and to download the referral form.

Montana

New Hope Pregnancy Clinic. Provides pregnancy testing, ultrasound examples, and counseling to help teens understand their options. Visit newhopemontana.org or call 1-406-723-7144.

Nevada

Community Pregnancy Center. Provides pregnant teens with educational, emotional, spiritual, and material support. Visit www.communitypregnancycenter.org or call 1-800-712-HELP for support and information.

New Hampshire

Options for Women. *Provides free* medical and counseling services as well as education and guidance to help both men and women make fully informed reproductive health decisions, including STD screening and testing, pregnancy and prenatal support, and after-abortion counseling for men and women age twenty-five and younger by appointment. Call 1-856-795-0048 for locations and to schedule an appointment.

New Jersey

Friendship Center for New Beginnings. Provides counseling to help teens understand their pregnancy options, pregnancy testing, and parenting and life skills courses. Visit friendship-center.org for more information.

New York

The Door. Provides comprehensive youth development services in a diverse and caring environment. Its mission is to empower young people to reach their potential. Check out their extensive programming at www.door.org/programs-services.

Inwood House. Provides programs, care, tools, and support to help teen parents overcome the statistics and build a successful life for themselves and their babies. Services include the Teen Family Learning Center, which provides a home, community, services, and support for teen moms in foster care and their babies; Victory House, which provides a home, community, services, and support for young women who are runaways or homeless pregnant and parenting moms and their babies; Mother-Child Foster Care, which recruits, places, and supports teen moms and their foster parents to help both provide stable, nurturing homes and permanent family connections; Fathers Count program for the fathers, which offers mentorship, career development, academic support, peer-to-peer community building; and Passport to Parenting courses to support pregnant and parenting teens. Visit inwoodhouse.com.previewdns.com/what-we-do/teen-family-support for more information.

North Carolina

Teens as Parents. Provides pregnant and parenting teens in Harnett County prenatal health care, parenting skills classes, and support to achieve educational goals. Services provided include weekly in-home visitation and support, monthly group meetings, and access to other programs. Visit teensasparents.com for more information.

North Dakota

The Perry Center for Unwed Mothers. Provides counseling, encouragement, classes, and a mentoring program to help teen mothers develop the skills they need to be successful parents. Visit perrycenter.org for more details and information.

Ohio

Madonna's Center. Provides support to teen parents at every stage of the pregnancy and parenting journey, from prenatal care to preschool and kindergarten classes for the children of teen parents. Visit www.madonnascenter.org/beta/?page_id=45 for more information.

Pennsylvania

Mary's Shelter. Provides residential and nonresidential services for pregnant women and women with newborns who are in need of a supportive environment because of a lack of suitable housing or favorable family relationships. While caring for women in need, Mary's Shelter prepares mothers with newborns for independent living and a vision of hope for the future. Visit marysshelter.org/index.php for more information.

South Carolina

The Jubilee Home for Pregnant and Teen Parents. Provides physical, spiritual, and emotional shelter for teen parents. Visit www.jubileeteen.com or call 1-803-464-7182 for more information.

Texas

Jane's Due Process. Provides legal representation for pregnant minors in Texas. Created in 2001, Jane's Due Process is recognized in parental involvement states as a pioneer in delivering legal services to pregnant teens. The core of the JDP program is its statewide toll-free legal hotline, lawyer referral program, and website. Call 1-866-WWW-JANE or visit janesdueprocess.org for more information.

Utah

Teen Mother and Child Program. Provides obstetric, pediatric, and adolescent health care (including family planning); acute crisis counseling and long-term counseling for the teen; vocational/educational counseling and tracking for teen parents; and nutrition counseling. Visit healthcare.utah.edu/pediatrics/general pediatrics/tmcp.html or call 1-801-468-3950 for more information.

Vermont

Sunrise Family Resource Center. Provides child care, secondary education, case management, advocacy and intensive home-based supports, resources and refer- ral for child care providers, employment counseling, and parenting education. Visit www.sunrisefamilyresourcecenter.com or call 1-802-442-6934 for more information.

Virginia

Resource Mothers Program. Provides mentoring services and support to pregnant teenagers up to the age of nineteen, from the prenatal period until the infant's first birthday. Visit www.vdh.virginia.gov/LHD/threeriv/ResourceMothers.htm for program eligibility and application process information.

Notes

Introduction

1. Kathryn Kost and Stanley Henshaw, *U.S. Teenage Pregnancies, Births and Abortions, 2010: National and State Trends by Age, Race and Ethnicity* (New York: Guttmacher Institute, 2014).
2. "A Letter to Teen Parents," StayTeen.org, n.d., stayteen.org/letter-teen-parents (accessed November 27, 2015).
3. "Support Safer Sex," MLNB, n.d., makelovenotbabies.com/support-safer-sex/ (accessed November 27, 2015), Teen Pregnancy Prevention, teenpregnancyprevention.tumblr.com/page/3 (accessed November 27, 2015), and "Birth Control," Teen Pregnancy," n.d., itsmyteensex lifebeinformed.weebly.com/birth-control.html (accessed November 27, 2015).
4. "Teen Pregnancy Basics," In the Know Zone, n.d., www.intheknowzone.com/mental-health -topics/teen-pregnancy.html (accessed November 27, 2015).

Chapter 1

1. Sammi, e-mail interview with author, May 6, 2014.
2. Sammi, e-mail interview.
3. Sammi, e-mail interview.
4. "Myth vs. Fact," StayTeen.org, n.d., stayteen.org/myths (accessed April 21, 2014).
5. Sammi, e-mail interview.
6. "Myth vs. Fact."
7. Sammi, e-mail interview.
8. Sammi, e-mail interview.
9. "The Ten Biggest Myths about Sex," Planned Parenthood, 2015, www.plannedparenthood .org/teens/sex/the-ten-biggest-myths-about-sex (November 30, 2015).
10. Sammi, e-mail interview.
11. "The Ten Biggest Myths about Sex."
12. "The Ten Biggest Myths about Sex."
13. "The Ten Biggest Myths about Sex."
14. "The Ten Biggest Myths about Sex."
15. Sammi, e-mail interview.
16. Sammi, e-mail interview.
17. Sammi, e-mail interview.
18. Sammi, e-mail interview.

---

a. S. A. Sanders, B. J. Hill, W. L. Yarber, C. A. Graham, R. A. Crosby, and R. R. Milhausen, "Misclassification Bias: Diversity in Conceptualisations about Having 'Had Sex,'" *Sexual Health* 7 (2010): 31–34, dx.doi.org/10.1071/SH09068 (accessed April 21, 2014).

b. Sanders et al., "Misclassification Bias."

c. Sanders et al., "Misclassification Bias."

d. *Merriam-Webster Online*, s.v. "Sex," www.merriam-webster.com/dictionary/sex (accessed April 21, 2014).

e. "Facts on American Teens' Sexual and Reproductive Health," Guttmacher Institute, June 2013, www.guttmacher.org/pubs/FB-ATSRH.html#23a (accessed April 21, 2014).

f. Kelleen Kaye, Jennifer Appleton Gootman, Alison Stewart Ng, and Cara Finley, *The Benefits of Birth Control in America: Getting the Facts Straight* (Washington, DC: National Campaign to Prevent Teen and Unplanned Pregnancy, 2014), thenationalcampaign.org/resource/benefits-birth-control (accessed April 21, 2014).

Chapter 2

1. "Definition of Embryo," MedicineNet.com, n.d., www.medicinenet.com/script/main/art.asp?articlekey=3225 (accessed August 20, 2015).

2. "Your Pregnancy: 2 Weeks," BabyCenter, n.d., www.babycenter.com/6_your-pregnancy-2-weeks_6000.bc (accessed March 25, 2015).

3. "Definition of Fetus," MedicineNet.com, n.d., www.medicinenet.com/script/main/art.asp?articlekey=3424 (accessed March 25, 2015).

4. Lambeth Hochwald, "A Cheat Sheet to Pregnancy Hormones," *Parents*, 2011, www.parents.com/pregnancy/my-life/emotions/understanding-pregnancy-hormones/ (accessed March 25, 2015).

5. "Definition of Hormone," MedicineNet.com, n.d., www.medicinenet.com/script/main/art.asp?articlekey=3783 (accessed March 25, 2015).

6. Hochwald, "A Cheat Sheet to Pregnancy Hormones."

7. "Conception & Pregnancy: Ovulation, Fertilization, and More," WebMD, August 18, 2014, www.webmd.com/baby/guide/understanding-conception?page=2 (accessed March 25, 2015).

8. *Merriam-Webster Online*, s.v. "Prenatal," www.merriam-webster.com/dictionary/prenatal (accessed March 25, 2015).

9. Tim Taylor, "Uterus," InnerBody, n.d., www.innerbody.com/image_repfov/repo11-new.html (accessed March 25, 2015).

10. "Missed or Irregular Periods," WebMD, last updated November 14, 2014, www.webmd.com/women/tc/missed-or-irregular-periods-topic-overview (accessed April 9, 2015).

11. "Missed or Irregular Periods."

12. Office on Women's Health in the Department of Health and Human Services, "Pregnancy Tests," WomensHealth.gov, last updated December 23, 2014, www.womenshealth.gov/publications/our-publications/fact-sheet/pregnancy-test.html#note1 (accessed April 14, 2015).

13. U.S. National Library of Medicine, "Pregnancy Test," MedlinePlus, last updated November 16, 2014, www.nlm.nih.gov/medlineplus/ency/article/003432.htm (accessed April 14, 2015).

14. Kara Corridan, "Tips for Taking an At-Home Pregnancy Test," *Parents*, 2015, www.parents.com/videos/v/70569199/tips-for-taking-an-at-home-pregnancy-test.htm (accessed April 9, 2015).

15. Dr. Charlene Gaebler-Uhing, interview with author, April 19, 2015.

16. Dr. Gaebler-Uhing, interview.
17. Melissa Vukovich, interview with author, June 3, 2015.
18. Dr. Gaebler-Uhing, interview.
19. Vukovich, interview.
20. Dr. Gaebler-Uhing, interview.
21. Vukovich, interview.
22. Dr. Gaebler-Uhing, interview.
23. Vukovich, interview.
24. Dr. Gaebler-Uhing, interview.
25. Vukovich, interview.
26. Vukovich, interview.
27. Vukovich, interview.
28. Dr. Gaebler-Uhing, interview.
29. Vukovich, interview.

a. Susan Ramin, "Morning Sickness: Causes, Concerns, Treatments," BabyCenter.com, n.d., www.babycenter.com/morning-sickness (accessed April 9, 2015).
b. Ramin, "Morning Sickness."
c. Ramin, "Morning Sickness."
d. William Lueck, interview with author, June 25, 2014. All of William's responses in this section come from the same interview.
e. Dr. Charlene Gaebler-Uhing, interview with author, April 19, 2015.
f. Melissa Vukovich, interview with author, June 3, 2015.
g. Vukovich, interview.
h. Dr. Gaebler-Uhing, interview.

Chapter 3

1. J. N. Giedd, "Development of the Human Corpus Callosum during Childhood and Adolescence: A Longitudinal MRI Study," Progress in Neuro-Psychopharmacology & Biological Psychiatry 23 (1999): 571–588.
2. A. Rae Simpson, "Brain Changes," MIT Young Adult Development Project, 2008, hrweb .mit.edu/worklife/youngadult/brain.html (accessed April 23, 2015).
3. Simpson, "Brain Changes."
4. Marla Tabaka, "Stop Avoiding Tough Conversations: 3 Ways," Inc., n.d., www.inc.com/ marla-tabaka/stop-avoiding-tough-conversations.html (accessed April 23, 2015).
5. "Let's Talk about Teenage Pregnancy—Breaking the News," Families.com, n.d., http:// www.families.com/blog/lets-talk-about-teenage-pregnancy-breaking-the-big-news (accessed April 20, 2015).
6. Stephen R. Covey, "The 7 Habits of Highly Effective People: Habit 5: Seek First to Understand, Then to Be Understood," StephenCovey.com, n.d., www.stephencovey .com/7habits/7habits-habit5.php (accessed May 6, 2015).
7. "Should You Wait until 12 Weeks to Share Your Pregnancy News?" FitPregnancy, n.d., www.fitpregnancy.com/pregnancy/labor-delivery/ask-labor-nurse/should-you-wait-until -12-weeks-share-your-pregnancy-news (accessed May 7, 2015).

8. Kathryn Matthews, "The Dear John Talk, and Other Dreaded Conversations," Oprah.com, n.d., www.oprah.com/spirit/How-to-Have-a-Difficult-Conversation-Delivering-Bad-News (accessed May 9, 2015).

9. Drew Coster, "Teenage Pregnancy: 10 Tips for Telling Your Parents," PsychCentral, n.d., psychcentral.com/blog/archives/2013/06/19/teenage-pregnancy-10-tips-for-telling-your-parents/ (accessed May 9, 2015).

a. A. Rae Simpson, "Changes in Young Adulthood," MIT Young Adult Development Project, 2008, hrweb.mit.edu/worklife/youngadult/changes_adolescence.html#text (accessed April 23, 2015).

b. Simpson, "Changes in Young Adulthood."

c. Pam, phone interview with author, September 2, 2015.

d. CJ, response to blog post on August 6, 2014, www.wiseteendad.com/16-and-pregnant/ (accessed April 20, 2015).

e. The Nemours Foundation, "Telling Parents You're Pregnant," TeensHealth, n.d., kidshealth.org/teen/your_mind/Parents/tell_parents.html (accessed April 30, 2015).

f. Judy Ringer, "We Have to Talk: A Step-by-Step Checklist for Difficult Conversations," JudyRinger.com, n.d., www.judyringer.com/resources/articles/we-have-to-talk-a-stepbystep-checklist-for-difficult-conversations.php (accessed May 6, 2015).

g. Mardie Caldwell, "Breaking the News to Your Parents: Help for Pregnant Teens," StreetDirectory.com, n.d., www.streetdirectory.com/travel_guide/202622/kids_and_teens/breaking_the_news_to_your_parents_help_for_pregnant_teens.html (accessed May 6, 2015).

h. Kathryn Matthews, "The Dear John Talk and Other Dreaded Conversations," Oprah.com, n.d., www.oprah.com/spirit/How-to-Have-a-Difficult-Conversation-Delivering-Bad-News (accessed May 9, 2015).

i. Thuy Yau, e-mail interview with author, April 10, 2015. All of Thuy's responses in this Q&A come from the same e-mail interview.

j. Thuy Yau, "Why Having Young Parents Can Add Meaning to Your Life," Lifehack.org, n.d., www.lifehack.org/articles/communication/20-reasons-why-having-young-parents-can-add-meaning-your-life.html (accessed May 9, 2015).

Chapter 4

1. Dr. Charlene Gaebler-Uhing, interview with author, April 19, 2015.

2. Sarah Grey, "What We Don't Talk about When We Don't Talk about Abortion," *Truthout*, July 11, 2014, www.truth-out.org/opinion/item/24846-what-we-dont-talk-about-when-we-dont-talk-about-abortion# (accessed May 11, 2015).

3. Shanemarks3, "10 Most Controversial Topics for 2014," Visually, February 9, 2014, visual.ly/10-most-controversial-topics-2014 (accessed May 11, 2015).

4. L. B. Finer and M. R. Zolna, "Shifts in Intended and Unintended Pregnancies in the United States, 2001–2008," *American Journal of Public Health* 23, no. 3 (2014): e1–e9.

5. R. K. Jones and J. Jerman, "Abortion Incidence and Service Availability in the United States, 2011," *Perspectives on Sexual and Reproductive Health* 46, no. 1 (2011): 3–14.

6. R. K. Jones, L. B. Finer, and S. Singh, *Characteristics of U.S. Abortion Patients, 2008* (New York: Guttmacher Institute, 2010).

7. Jones et al., *Characteristics of U.S. Abortion Patients, 2008*.
8. "Induced Abortion in the United States," Guttmacher Institute, July 2014, www.guttmacher .org/pubs/fb_induced_abortion.html#6a (accessed May 12, 2015).
9. "Induced Abortion in the United States."
10. "The Abortion Pill at a Glance," Planned Parenthood, 2014, www.plannedparenthood.org/ learn/abortion/the-abortion-pill#sthash.MFWHSDOJ.dpuf (accessed May 12, 2015).
11. "What Is an Abortion," 1 in 3 Campaign, n.d., www.1in3campaign.org/resources/abortion -information-resources (accessed May 12, 2015).
12. "In-Clinic Abortion Procedures," Planned Parenthood, 2014, www.plannedparenthood.org/ learn/abortion/in-clinic-abortion-procedures (accessed May 12, 2015).
13. "In-Clinic Abortion Procedures."
14. "In-Clinic Abortion Procedures."
15. Poem featured in the author Jessica Akin's master's memoir thesis, *Voices*.
16. "Induced Abortion in the United States."
17. Heather D. Boonstra, Rachel Benson Gold, Cory L. Richards, and Lawrence B. Finer, *Abortion in Women's Lives* (New York: Guttmacher Institute, 2006), www.guttmacher.org/ pubs/2006/05/04/AiWL.pdf (accessed May 12, 2015).
18. B. Major et al., *Report of the Task Force on Mental Health and Abortion* (Washington, DC: American Psychological Association Task Force on Mental Health and Abortion, 2008), www .apa.org/pi/wpo/mental-health-abortion-report.pdf (accessed April 19, 2010).
19. "What Birth Parents Should Know about Adoption," EnlightenMe, 2015, enlightenme.com/ birth-parents-know-adoption/ (accessed May 18, 2015).
20. "Deciding between Abortion or Adoption," American Adoptions, 2015, www.american adoptions.com/pregnant/deciding_between_abortion_or_adoption (accessed May 12, 2015).
21. "Top Ten Interesting Adoption Facts," EnlightenMe, 2015, enlightenme.com/facts -adoption/ (accessed May 18, 2015).
22. "Facts and Statistics," Congressional Coalition on Adoption Institute, 2011, ccainstitute.org/ index.php?option=com_content&view=category&id=25&layout=blog&Itemid=43 (accessed May 20, 2015).
23. Alison Stewart Ng and Kelleen Kayne, "Teen Childbearing, Single Parenthood, and Father Involvement," *Why It Matters*, October 2012, thenationalcampaign.org/sites/default/files/ resource-primary-download/childbearing-singleparenthood-fatherinvolvement.pdf (accessed May 12, 2015).
24. K. S. Howard, J. E Burke Lefever, J. G. Borkowski, and T. L. Whitman, "Fathers' Influence in the Lives of Children with Adolescent Mothers," *Journal of Family Psychology* 2012, 468–476.
25. Christine Winquist Nord and Jerry West, *Fathers' and Mothers' Involvement in Their Children's Schools by Family Type and Resident Status* (Washington, DC: U.S. Department of Education, National Center for Education Statistics, 2001), nces.ed.gov/pubs2001/2001032.pdf (accessed May 22, 2015).
26. The National Campaign to Prevent Teen and Unplanned Pregnancy, "Teen Childbearing, Education, and Economic Wellbeing," *Why It Matters*, July 2012, thenationalcampaign.org/ sites/default/files/resource-primary-download/childbearing-education-economicwellbeing .pdf (accessed May 22, 2015).
27. "First-Year Baby Costs Calculator," BabyCenter.com, 2015, www.babycenter.com/baby -cost-calculator (accessed May 22, 2015).

28. "Counting It Up: The Public Costs of Teen Childbearing," the National Campaign to Prevent Teen and Unplanned Pregnancy, 2010, thenationalcampaign.org/why-it-matters/public-cost (accessed May 22, 2015).

29. "11 Facts about Teen Pregnancy," DoSomething.org, 2015, www.dosomething.org/facts/11 -facts-about-teen-pregnancy (accessed May 22, 2015).

30. "American Teens Sexual and Reproductive Health," Guttmacher Institute, May 2014, www .guttmacher.org/pubs/FB-ATSRH.html (accessed May 22, 2015).

a. Isabel, "Pregnancy and Birth Story," Pregnancy.com, n.d., www.pregnancy.com.au/resources/ birth-stories/teenage_stories/pregnancy-and-birth-story-2.shtml (accessed May 9, 2015).

b. Anonymous, "Fifteen with Twins," Pregnancy.com, n.d., www.pregnancy.com.au/resources/ birth-stories/teenage_stories/fifteen-with-twins.shtml (accessed May 9, 2015).

c. "Talkline," Backline, n.d., yourbackline.org/find-support/talkline/ (accessed May 11, 2015).

d. *Dictionary.com*, s.v. "abortion," dictionary.reference.com/browse/abortion (accessed May 12, 2015).

e. "In-Clinic Abortion Procedures at a Glance," Planned Parenthood, 2014, www.planned parenthood.org/learn/abortion/in-clinic-abortion-procedures (accessed May 12, 2014).

f. "Top 10 Interesting Adoption Facts," EnlightenMe, 2015, enlightenme.com/facts-adoption/ (accessed May 18, 2015).

g. "The 5 W's of Adoption," AdoptionServices, Inc., 2015, www.adoptionservicesinc.com/The -5-Ws-of-Adoption.html (accessed May 18, 2015).

h. Ann Angel, interview with author, May 28, 2015. All of Ann's responses in this Q&A come from the same e-mail interview.

i. "The 5 W's of Adoption."

j. "Financial Assistance for Pregnancy-Related Expenses," American Adoptions, 2015, www .americanadoptions.com/pregnant/article_view/article_id/4415?cId=177 (accessed May 20, 2015).

k. "Top 10 Interesting Adoption Facts."

l. Amanda Angel, e-mail interview with author, May 31, 2015. All of Amanda's responses in this Q&A come from the same e-mail interview.

m. Mark Lowrance, "My Girlfriend Is Pregnant?!" WiseTeenDad, 2015, www.wiseteendad. com/my-girlfriend-is-pregnant/ (accessed May 20, 2015).

n. "11 Facts about Teen Dads," DoSomething.org, n.d., www.dosomething.org/facts/11-facts -about-teen-dads (accessed May 22, 2015).

Chapter 5

1. Abby K., "Judgement of Teen Moms," *Teen Ink*, www.teenink.com/hot_topics/what_ matters/article/340717/Judgement-of-Teen-Moms/ (accessed May 26, 2015).

2. "Making the Case for Wanted and Welcomed Pregnancy," the National Campaign to Prevent Teen and Unplanned Pregnancy, 2015, thenationalcampaign.org/why-it-matters (accessed May 26, 2015).

3. Ice Cube, "Check Yo Self," www.azlyrics.com/lyrics/icecube/checkyoself.html (accessed May 27, 2015).

4. Jane Collingwood, "The Importance of Personal Boundaries," PsychCentral, 2013, psych-central.com/lib/the-importance-of-personal-boundaries/ (accessed May 29, 2015).

5. "Crisis Symptoms, Causes and Effects," PsychGuides.com, n.d., www.psychguides.com/ guides/crisis-symptoms-causes-and-effects/ (accessed June 2, 2015).

6. "The Pregnant Teen's Dilemma," Focus on the Family, 2015, www.focusonthefamily.com/ lifechallenges/love-and-sex/abortion/your-daughters-experience (accessed June 2, 2015).

7. Sian Beilock, "The Power of Expressing Yourself," *Psychology Today*, September 19, 2012, www.psychologytoday.com/blog/choke/201209/the-power-expressing-yourself (accessed June 2, 2015).

8. John M. Grohol, "15 Common Defense Mechanisms," PsychCentral, January 30, 2013, psychcentral.com/lib/15-common-defense-mechanisms/ (accessed June 2, 2015).

9. "Denial of Pregnancy," Pregnancy to Baby, 2008, www.pregnancytobaby.com/category/ during-pregnancy/denial-of-pregnancy/ (accessed June 2, 2015).

10. Barbara Laker, "Babies Hiding Babies Combating the Denial Many Teens Hide Their Pregnancies, to No Avail," *Philly.com*, January 15, 1997, articles.philly.com/1997-01-15/ news/25559831_1_amy-grossberg-teen-mom-pregnancy (accessed June 2, 2015).

11. "The Pregnant Teen's Dilemma."

12. "How Adolescent Parenting Affects Children, Families, and Communities," the Urban Child Institute, February 27, 2014, www.urbanchildinstitute.org/articles/editorials/how -adolescent-parenting-affects-children-families-and-communities (accessed May 27, 2015).

13. "11 Facts about Teen Pregnancy," DoSomething.org, 2015, www.dosomething.org/facts/11- facts-about-teen-pregnancy (accessed June 2, 2015).

14. Kelleen Kaye, Jennifer Appleton Gootman, Alison Stewart Ng, and Cara Finley, *The Benefits of Birth Control in America: Getting the Facts Straight* (Washington, DC: National Campaign to Prevent Teen and Unplanned Pregnancy, 2014), thenationalcampaign.org/resource/ benefits-birth-control (accessed April 21, 2014).

15. Kaye et al., *The Benefits of Birth Control in America.*

16. Kaye et al., *The Benefits of Birth Control in America.*

a. Leo Babauta, "The Art of Handling Criticism Gracefully," Aen Habits, March 21, 2011, zenhabits.net/criticism/ (accessed May 26, 2015).

b. Chelsea H., "Guilt about Being a Teen Mom," BabyCenter.com, August 11, 2011, community.babycenter.com/post/a28924935/guilt_about_being_a_teen_mom (accessed October 13, 2015).

c. Kate Walker, "My Teenage Daughter Is Pregnant—I Feel So Ashamed," *Guardian*, October 21, 2011, www.theguardian.com/lifeandstyle/2011/oct/22/teenage-pregnancy-shame -mother-daughter (accessed September 30, 2015).

d. Deborah Bloom, "Forest Grove High-Schooler Fakes Pregnancy for Senior Project on Stereotyping," *OregonLive*, April 16, 2013, www.oregonlive.com/forest-grove/index.ssf/2013/04/ forest_grove_high_schooler_fak.html (accessed October 13, 2015).

e. John Preston, "How Can I Manage Feelings of Guilt and Shame When I Am Depressed?" ShareCare, 2015, www.sharecare.com/health/depression-living-with/how-manage-guilt -shame-depressed (accessed June 2, 2015).

f. Frank Newport, "Americans, Including Catholics, Say Birth Control Is Morally OK," Gallup, May 22, 2012, www.gallup.com/poll/154799/americans-including-catholics-say-birth -control-morally.aspx (accessed June 2, 2015).

g. R. K. Jones and J. Dreweke, *Countering Conventional Wisdom: New Evidence on Religion and Contraceptive Use* (New York: Guttmacher Institute, 2011), www.guttmacher.org/pubs/ Religion-and-Contraceptive-Use.pdf (accessed April 21, 2014)

h. "This Week's Activity," BabyCenter.com, 2015, www.babycenter.com/6_your-pregnancy -10-weeks_1099.bc#articlesection4 (accessed April 20, 2015).

Chapter 6

1. "Know the Facts," Teens for Life, 2009, www.teensforlife.com/be-informed/know-the-facts/ (accessed May 20, 2015).
2. Stephen M. R. Covey and Rebecca R. Merrill, *The Speed of Trust: The One Thing That Changes Everything* (New York: Free Press, 2006), 215.
3. Covey and Merrill, *The Speed of Trust*, 215.
4. Covey and Merrill, *The Speed of Trust*, 220.
5. Covey and Merrill, *The Speed of Trust*, 220.
6. Kathryn Hatter, "How Teens Build Trust with Parents," ModernMom, 2015, motherhood .modernmom.com/teens-build-trust-parents-6182.html (accessed June 11, 2015).
7. Eileen Kennedy-Moore, "Make New Friends but Keep the Old . . . or Not," *Psychology Today*, May 24, 2012, www.psychologytoday.com/blog/growing-friendships/201205/make -new-friends-keep-the-old-or-not (accessed June 11, 2015).
8. Kennedy-Moore, "Make New Friends but Keep the Old . . . or Not."
9. Kennedy-Moore, "Make New Friends but Keep the Old . . . or Not."
10. Kennedy-Moore, "Make New Friends but Keep the Old . . . or Not."
11. Kennedy-Moore, "Make New Friends but Keep the Old . . . or Not."
12. Jessica Stevenson, "Eight Easy Ways to Make New Friends and Meet People," About.com, 2015, teenadvice.about.com/od/datingrelationships/tp/making-new-friends.htm (accessed June 11, 2015).
13. Stevenson, "Eight Easy Ways to Make New Friends and Meet People."
14. Stevenson, "Eight Easy Ways to Make New Friends and Meet People."
15. Stevenson, "Eight Easy Ways to Make New Friends and Meet People."
16. "American Teens Sexual and Reproductive Health," Guttmacher Institute, June 2014, www .guttmacher.org/pubs/FB-ATSRH.html (accessed June 15, 2015).
17. Alison Stewart Ng and Kelleen Kaye, "Teen Childbearing, Single Parenthood, and Father Involvement," *Why It Matters*, October 2012, thenationalcampaign.org/sites/default/files/ resource-primary-download/childbearing-singleparenthood-fatherinvolvement.pdf (accessed June 15, 2015).
18. Edward Kruk, "What Exactly Is 'The Best Interest of the Child'?" *Psychology Today*, February 22, 2015, www.psychologytoday.com/blog/co-parenting-after-divorce/201502/what -exactly-is-the-best-interest-the-child (accessed June 17, 2015).
19. Kruk, "What Exactly Is 'The Best Interest of the Child'?"
20. Jocelyn Block and Melinda Smith, "Co-Parenting Tips for Divorced Parents," HelpGuide .org, July 2015, www.helpguide.org/articles/family-divorce/co-parenting-tips-for-divorced -parents.htm (accessed June 20, 2015).

a. Daizchane Baker, "An Intimate Look at Life as a Teen Mom," *Teen Vogue*, January 27, 2014, www.teenvogue.com/my-life/2014-01/teen-mom (accessed June 10, 2015).
b. "This Week's Activity," BabyCenter.com, 2015, www.babycenter.com/6_your-pregnancy -11-weeks_1100.bc#articlesection4 (accessed April 20, 2015).

c. Todd Smith, "Is Your Word Really Your Bond?" *Little Things Matter* (blog), 2013, www
    .littlethingsmatter.com/blog/2010/08/09/is-your-word-really-your-bond/ (accessed June 11,
    2015).

d. C. S. Lewis, *The Four Loves* (New York: Harcourt, Brace, 1960), 65.

e. Mark Lowrance, e-mail interview with author, July, 2, 2015. All of Mark's responses in this
    section come from the same e-mail interview.

f. Department of Social Services, *Establishing Paternity* (New Haven, CT: Public and Government
    Relations Office, 2007), www.ct.gov/dss/lib/dss/pdfs/dadbklt.pdf (accessed July 21, 2014).

g. "This Week's Activity," BabyCenter.com, 2015, www.babycenter.com/6_your-pregnancy
    -12-weeks_1101.bc (accessed June 20, 2015).

Chapter 7

1. The National Campaign to Prevent Teen and Unplanned Pregnancy, "Teen Childbearing,
    Education, and Economic Wellbeing," *Why It Matters*, July 2012, thenationalcampaign.org/
    sites/default/files/resource-primary-download/childbearing-education-economicwellbeing
    .pdf (accessed April 20, 2015).

2. Carla Amurao, "Fact Sheet: Is the Dropout Problem Real?" PBS.org, February 21, 2013,
    www.pbs.org/wnet/tavissmiley/tsr/education-under-arrest/fact-sheet-drop-out-rates-of
    -african-american-boys/ (accessed April 20, 2015).

3. Jennifer Cheeseman Day and Eric C. Newburger, "The Big Payoff: Educational Attainment
    and Synthetic Estimates of Work-Life Earnings," United States Census Bureau, July 2002,
    www.census.gov/prod/2002pubs/p23-210.pdf (accessed April 20, 2015).

4. J. R. Pleis, B. W. Ward, and J. W. Lucas, "Summary Health Statistics for U.S. Adults: National
    Health Interview Survey, 2009," CDC.gov, December 2010, www.cdc.gov/nchs/data/series/
    sr_10/sr10_249.pdf (accessed April 20, 2015).

5. Christina Couch, "Two-Year vs. Four-Year Colleges: Which One Is Right For You?" Col-
    legeView.com, n.d., www.collegeview.com/articles/article/two-year-vs-four-year-colleges
    -which-one-is-right-for-you (accessed April 20, 2015).

6. "Average Published Undergraduate Charges by Sector," CollegeBoard.org, 2014–2015,
    trends.collegeboard.org/college-pricing/figures-tables/average-published-undergraduate
    -charges-sector-2014-15 (accessed June 23, 2015).

7. "Average Published Undergraduate Charges by Sector."

a. "This Week's Activity," BabyCenter.com, 2015, www.babycenter.com/6_your-pregnancy
    -13-weeks_1102.bc (accessed April 20, 2015).

b. Holly Hagaman, interview with author, February 20, 2015.

c. Hagaman, interview. All of Holly's responses in this Q&A come from the same interview.

Chapter 8

1. Kelleen Kaye, "Teen Childbearing and Infant Health," *Why It Matters*, October 2012,
    thenationalcampaign.org/sites/default/files/resource-primary-download/childbearing-infant
    -health.pdf (accessed June 23, 2015).

2. Kaye, "Teen Childbearing and Infant Health."

3. "Teenage Pregnancy," March of Dimes, July 2012, www.marchofdimes.org/materials/teen-age-pregnancy.pdf (accessed June 29, 2015).

4. BabyCenter Medical Advisory Board, "Preeclampsia," BabyCenter.com, September 2014, www.babycenter.com/0_preeclampsia_257.bc?showAll=true (accessed June 29, 2015).

5. Kaye, "Teen Childbearing and Infant Health."

6. "What We Know about Prematurity," March of Dimes, 2012, www.marchofdimes.com/mission/prematurity_indepth.html (accessed June 29, 2015).

7. Kecia Gaither, "Health and Pregnancy," WebMD, September 14, 2014, www.webmd.com/baby/guide/teen-pregnancy-medical-risks-and-realities?page=3 (accessed June 29, 2015).

8. BabyCenter Medical Advisory Board, "Miscarriage: The Signs, Causes, Treatment, and How to Cope," BabyCenter.com, May 2015, www.babycenter.com/0_miscarriage-the-signs-causes-treatment-and-how-to-cope_252.bc (accessed June 29, 2015).

9. Sharon Perkins, "Teenagers & Miscarriage," LiveStrong.com, August 16, 2013, www.livestrong.com/article/1001078-teenagers-miscarriage/ (accessed June 30, 2015).

10. "Miscarriage," March of Dimes, July 2012, www.marchofdimes.org/loss/miscarriage.aspx (accessed June 30, 2015).

11. "Miscarriage."

12. "Miscarriage."

13. Kaye, "Teen Childbearing and Infant Health."

14. Mayo Clinic Staff, "Pregnancy Diet: Focus on These Essential Nutrients," Mayo Clinic, March 1, 2014, www.mayoclinic.org/healthy-lifestyle/pregnancy-week-by-week/in-depth/pregnancy-nutrition/art-20045082 (accessed June 29, 2015).

15. Trina Pagano, "Smoking during Pregnancy," WebMD, May 30, 2014, www.webmd.com/baby/smoking-during-pregnancy?page=2 (accessed June 29, 2015).

16. "Smoking, Alcohol and Drugs," March of Dimes, July 2012, www.marchofdimes.org/pregnancy/alcohol-during-pregnancy.aspx (accessed June 29, 2015).

17. "Smoking, Alcohol and Drugs."

18. "Smoking, Alcohol and Drugs."

19. The BabyCenter Editorial Team, "Is It Safe to Dye My Hair during Pregnancy?" BabyCenter.com, 2015, www.babycenter.com/404_is-it-safe-to-dye-my-hair-during-pregnancy_3273.bc (accessed July 1, 2015).

20. Stacey Stapleton, "Is It Safe to Tan during Pregnancy?" Parents.com, 2015, www.parents.com/advice/pregnancy-birth/my-pregnant-body/is-it-safe-to-tan-during-pregnancy/ (accessed July 1, 2015).

21. "Pregnancy and Exercise," Better Health Channel, January 2014, www.betterhealth.vic.gov.au/bhcv2/bhcarticles.nsf/pages/Pregnancy_and_exercise (accessed July 1, 2015).

22. "Tattoos When Pregnant," American Pregnancy Association, July 2015, americanpregnancy.org/pregnancy-health/tattoos/ (accessed July 1, 2015).

23. "Piercing and Pregnancy: Safety and Health Risks," American Pregnancy Association, July 2015, americanpregnancy.org/pregnancy-health/piercing-and-pregnancy/ (accessed July 1, 2015).

a. "Signs of Preterm Labor," March of Dimes, October 2013, www.marchofdimes.org/complications/signs-and-symptoms-of-preterm-labor-and-what-to-do.aspx (accessed June 29, 2015).

b.   Hannah, "Poem," Teen Miscarriage Community on LiveJournal, June 17, 2005, teenmiscarriage.livejournal.com/ (accessed July 1, 2015).

c.   Shona, "Untitled," Teen Miscarriage Community on LiveJournal, July 31, 2005, teenmiscarriage.livejournal.com/ (accessed June 29, 2015).

d.   "This Week's Activity," BabyCenter.com, 2015, www.babycenter.com/6_your-pregnancy -14-weeks_1103.bc#articlesection4 (accessed April 20, 2015).

e.   Tara LaBerge, e-mail interview with author, June 2, 2015. All of Tara's responses in this Q&A come from the same e-mail interview.

f.   "This Week's Activity," BabyCenter.com, 2015, www.babycenter.com/6_your-pregnancy -15-weeks_1104.bc#articlesection4 (accessed April 20, 2015).

Chapter 9

1.   Monica Meyer, e-mail interview with author, June 17, 2015.

2.   Meyer, e-mail interview.

3.   Meyer, e-mail interview.

4.   Meyer, e-mail interview.

5.   Thomas C., "Life as a Teen-Father-to-Be," 2014, www.youthsuccessnyc.org/sexuality/ stories/TeenFatherToBe-Thomas.html (accessed July 1, 2015).

6.   Thomas C., "Life as a Teen-Father-to-Be."

7.   Littleboyblue16, "I Am a Teenage Parent," Experience Project, August 5, 2009, www .experienceproject.com/stories/Am-A-Teenage-Parent/647908 (accessed July 1, 2015).

8.   David, "David's Story," Washingteen Help, n.d., washingteenhelp.org/pregnancy/david -story (accessed July 1, 2015).

9.   "The Science of Character," Let It Ripple, n.d., www.letitripple.org/character (accessed July 2, 2015).

10. Tom Rath and Marcus Buckingham, *StrengthsFinder 2.0* (New York: Gallup, 2007).

11. Mark Lowrance, e-mail interview with author, July 2, 2015.

a.   "This Week's Activity," BabyCenter.com, 2015, www.babycenter.com/6_your-pregnancy -17-weeks_1106.bc (accessed April 20, 2015).

b.   Monica Meyer, e-mail interview with, author June 17, 2015. All of Monica's responses in this Q&A come from the same e-mail interview.

c.   Meyer, e-mail interview.

d.   "This Week's Activity," BabyCenter.com, 2015, www.babycenter.com/6_your-pregnancy -18-weeks_1107.bc (accessed April 20, 2015).

e.   Barbara Bell, interview with author, June 6, 2015.

f.   Bell, interview.

g.   Bell, interview. All of Barbara's responses in this Q&A come from the same interview.

h.   "Bathing an Infant," MedlinePlus, April 14, 2014, www.nlm.nih.gov/medlineplus/ency/ patientinstructions/000020.htm (accessed July 3, 2015).

Resources

This resource list offers a selection of fiction and nonfiction books and movies to help teens learn more about being parents. Some of the listings are included to provide a different view or perspective on being a teen parent and help teens start a conversation with family and friends about teen parenting.

Movies

Coal Miner's Daughter (1980). This is an oldie but goodie and worth the watch. This biography of Loretta Lynn—one of the biggest country music legends of all time—profiles her life and the struggles and joys she faced marrying at fifteen, having four kids before she was twenty, and becoming a parent of a teen parent at twenty-nine. Produced by Universal Pictures, available online and via DVD, and runs 124 minutes.

For Keeps (1988). Don't let the year this movie was released stop you from watching it. Darcy Elliot and Stan Bobrucz are young, smart, and ambitious high school seniors focused on college and their futures. Then, they find out they are pregnant. Deciding against abortion or adoption, they decide to have the baby, raise it themselves, and get married. Feeling like they have all the answers soon leads them to realize they are completely unprepared, but still willing to work through the unknown together. Produced by TriStar Pictures and ML Delphi Premier Productions, available online and via DVD, and runs 90 minutes.

Juno (2007). *Juno* follows the story of a young girl, Juno, faced with an unexpected pregnancy. Juno grapples with the decision of whether to keep the baby and then, once she decides to keep the baby, whether to move forward with adoption. With the help of supportive parents and friends, Juno starts to understand herself better, which helps her make decisions regarding the baby and her future. Produced by Fox Searchlight Pictures, Mandate Pictures, and Mr. Mudd, available online and via DVD, and runs 96 minutes.

Knocked Up (2007). After a drunken one-night stand, a slacker learns that his partner from that night, a career girl, is pregnant, and together the two must deal with the repercussions. Although this movie isn't about teen pregnancy, it does cover many of the issues teens face—being unprepared, not knowing how to support themselves and baby, and figuring out how to co-parent when they aren't in a relationship with the person they had a baby with. Produced by Universal Pictures and Apatow Productions, available online and via DVD, and runs 129 minutes.

Precious (2009). Sixteen-year-old Precious is an overweight, abused teenager with one mentally challenged child she isn't in contact with when she finds herself pregnant with a second child. This is a story about overcoming challenges and impossible odds to become a better person and parent. Produced by Lionsgate, Lee Daniels Entertainment, and Smokewood Entertainment Group, available online and via DVD, and runs 110 minutes.

The Pregnancy Pact (2010). This movie is based on the allegedly true story of a 2008 media circus surrounding teenagers in Gloucester, Massachusetts, who allegedly agreed to concurrently give birth and raise their children communally. Produced by Von Zerneck Sertner Films, available online and via DVD, and runs 87 minutes.

Saved (2004). A good Christian teen finds herself in the family way after having sex with her boyfriend to save him from homosexuality. This movie profiles how difficult high school friendships can be and the importance of believing in oneself. Produced by United Artists, Single Cell Pictures, Infinity Media, James Forsyth Casting, and Red Bull Productions, available online and via DVD, and runs 92 minutes.

Stephanie Daley (2006). Stephanie Daley is a sixteen-year-old girl who collapses in a puddle of blood on a school field trip. A doctor later confirms she has recently given birth. That same day, a newborn baby is found dead, flushed down a toilet with its mouth stuffed with toilet paper, at the same location where Stephanie collapsed. The teen finds herself charged with killing the infant. Produced by RedBone Films and Silverwood Films, available online and via DVD, and runs 92 minutes.

Fiction Books

Sometimes reading novels about people in similar situations can help teens cope better with the situations they find themselves in—especially if they don't have an expansive network where they are connected with other young parents. The following books all deal with various teen pregnancy themes.

Amy Efaw, *After* (New York: Penguin Young Readers Group, 2010). Seemingly perfect and totally in control of her life, Devon finds her world unraveling when she's found by the police lying on her family sofa, bloody after giving birth to a baby who was found in a Dumpster. The story moves through Devon's arrest, her confusion about what is happening to her, and the court's decision on her actions.

Angela Johnson, *The First Part Last* (New York: Simon & Schuster Books for Young Readers, 2010). Written from the male side of teen pregnancy, main character Bobby finds himself desperate to do the right thing by his pregnant girlfriend and baby on the way.

Barbara Delinsky, *Not My Daughter* (New York: Anchor, 2010). The stories and struggles of a town and the mothers of three smart, popular teenage girls who make a pact to become pregnant and raise their babies together.

Catherine Greenman, *Hooked* (New York: Northfield Publishing, 2011). High school senior Thea Galehouse finds herself in love and then pregnant. A story about two teens attempting to stay together despite the challenges of raising a family, finishing school and going to college, and dealing with the inevitable challenges life brings.

Ellen Hopkins, *Crank* (New York: Margaret K. McElderry Books, 2013). This is a semi-autobiographical novel in verse about Kristina's struggle with addiction. Raped by her drug dealers, Kristina decides to keep the baby. While this decision slows her drug use, it doesn't stop it, and the story follows Kristina as she attempts to both parent and get clean.

Han Nolan, *Pregnant Pause* (New York: Harcourt, 2012). Sixteen-year-old Eleanor finds herself pregnant and confronted with two options: move to Kenya with her parents or get married to the baby's father. She chooses to stay and get married, and the story follows her as she struggles as a new wife, parent, and developing herself as a person.

Jo Knowles, *Jumping Off Swings* (Sommerville, MA: Candlewick Press, 2011). Written from the point of view of four characters, this novel explores the relationship Ellie, who finds herself pregnant after sleeping with many different men because it makes her feel good, has with the baby's father and their best friends.

Megan McCafferty, *Bumped* (New York: Balzer + Bray, 2012). A futuristic take on teen pregnancy where everyone over the age of eighteen is incapable of reproducing and would-be parents desperately bid for "conception contracts" with the prettiest, healthiest, and smartest girls—cash, college tuition, and liposuction in exchange for a baby. Main character Melody finds herself in a highly desirable situation but must make a decision: morality or money?

Pat Brisson, *The Best and Hardest Thing* (New York: Viking, 2010). A novel set in verse, this story follows fifteen-year-old Molly Biden, who has always been the practical, good, and upstanding girl people wanted her to be, until she meets Grady Dillon and ends up pregnant. The story covers her struggle to accept her pregnancy and the fact that her life will never be the same.

Sarah Dessen, *Someone like You* (New York: Puffin Books, 2004). The story of two best friends, Halley and Scarlett, who find their friendship tested and strengthened when Halley finds out she is pregnant and then loses the father of her child when he dies in a motorcycle accident.

Nonfiction Books

Following are several nonfiction books that can help educate teens on parenting, co-parenting, and understanding key developmental milestones.

Adele Faber and Elaine Mazlish, *How to Talk So Kids Will Listen & Listen So Kids Will Talk* (New York: Scribner, 2012). This book offers solutions to common problems and helps parents build foundations for lasting relationships. It includes insight on coping with a child's negative feelings, such as frustration, anger, and disappointment, how to express strong feelings without being hurtful, how to get a child's willing cooperation, and how to understand the difference between helpful and unhelpful praise.

Gaby Rodriguez, *The Pregnancy Project* (New York: Simon & Schuster Books, 2013). Enraged by the negative statistics and stereotypes teen mothers often face, this memoir is the firsthand account of author Gaby Rodriguez's experiences with—and what she learned from—faking her own pregnancy.

Harley Rotbart, MD, *No Regrets Parenting: Turning Long Days and Short Years into Cherished Moments with Your Kids* (New York: Andrews McMeel Publishing, 2012). *No Regrets Parenting* teaches parents how to experience the joy and depth of the parenting experience amidst the chaos and choreography of daily routines. Car pool, bath time, soccer practice, homework, dinner hour, and sleepovers all become more than just obligations and hurdles to overcome to get through the day. They are opportunities for intimate and meaningful time—quality time—with young kids. It's not how much time parents have with their kids, but how they spend that time that matters in the life and legacy of a young family.

Isolina Ricci, *Mom's House, Dad's House: Making Two Homes for Your Child* (New York: Touchstone, 1997). This book helps children heal and find a sense of continuity, security, and stability throughout the divorce process and in any custody situation. Includes examples, self-tests, checklists, tools, and guidelines to help separated moms and dads with the legal, emotional, and financial issues they will encounter as they work to create happy and stable homes.

Mariah Bruehl, *Playful Learning: Develop Your Child's Sense of Joy and Wonder* (New York: Roost Books, 2011). *Playful Learning* provides parents with easy-to-implement, hands-on projects in which they can engage their child in fun and creative ways that encourage learning and impart the joy of discovery. With a little bit of information and forethought, parents can play a pivotal role in the cognitive and creative development of their child.

Noël Janis-Norton, *Calmer, Easier, Happier Parenting: Five Strategies That End the Daily Battles and Get Kids to Listen the First Time* (New York: Plume, 2013). Based on her forty-plus years of experience, behavioral specialist Noël Janis-Norton outlines a clear, step-by-step plan of five strategies that will help any parent raise a child who is cooperative and considerate, confident, and self-reliant:

Descriptive Praise, Preparing for Success, Reflective Listening, Never Ask Twice, and Rewards and Consequences.

Dr. Pamela Douglas, *The Discontented Little Baby Book* (New York: University of Queensland Press, 2013). *The Discontented Little Baby Book* gives parents practical and evidence-based strategies for helping them and their baby get more in synch. With advice on dealing with feelings of anxiety and depression, and answers to questions about reflux and allergies, this book offers a revolutionary new approach to caring for baby.

Pamela Druckerman, *Bringing Up Bebe: One American Mother Discovers the Wisdom of French Parenting* (New York: Penguin Books, 2014). When American journalist Pamela Druckerman had a baby in Paris, she started noticing differences in how the French parented versus Americans, including eating, sleeping, and play habits and behaviors. This memoir covers her firsthand experiences and research and offers a humorous and witty take on traditional parenting books.

Penelope Leach, *Your Baby and Child: From Birth to Age Five* (New York: Knopf, 2010). This book describes, in easy-to-follow stages from birth through starting school, how children develop: what they are doing, experiencing, and feeling. She tackles both the questions parents often ask (What does a new baby's wakefulness or a toddler's tantrum mean?) and those that are more difficult (How should new parents time their return to work, choose day care, tell a child about a new baby or an impending divorce?). *Your Baby and Child* provides parents with the information, encouragement, and reassurance they need.

Ross W. Green, *The Explosive Child* (New York: Harper Paperbacks, 2014). This book offers constructive advice and strategies to deal with some of the most destructive childhood behaviors like screaming, swearing, crying, hitting, kicking, spitting, and biting. Dr. Ross Greene helps parents understand why and when children do these things and how to respond in ways that are nonpunitive, nonadversarial, humane, and effective.

Thomas W. Phelan, PhD, *1-2-3 Magic: Effective Discipline for Children 2–12* (New York: Parentmagic, 2010). The award-winning 1-2-3 Magic program addresses the difficult task of child discipline without arguing, yelling, or spanking. By means of three easy-to-follow steps, parents learn to manage troublesome behavior, encourage good behavior, and strengthen the parent-child relationship. Ten strategies for building a child's self-esteem and the six types of testing and manipulation a parent can expect from the child are discussed, as well as tips on how to prevent homework arguments, make mealtimes more enjoyable, conduct effective family meetings, and encourage children to start doing their household chores.

Index

About the Author

Jessica Akin was most recently the head of marketing and communications for the $450 billion trust and custody division of U.S. Bank. Akin writes full time and holds an MA in English with an emphasis on poetry from Mount Mary University. Teen pregnancy holds a special place in her heart, as her brother had a baby at eighteen when his girlfriend was sixteen. She hopes every teen going through the scary possibility, or reality, of an unplanned pregnancy has the support and love he or she needs to thrive.